IMAGINING
NIAGARA

IMAGINING NIAGARA

The Meaning

and

Making of

Niagara Falls

PATRICK V. McGREEVY

UNIVERSITY OF MASSACHUSETTS PRESS

Amherst

Copyright © 1994 b

The University of Massachu   tts Press

All rights reserved

Printed in the United States of America

ISBN 0–87023–916–3

LC 93–35720

Designed by Teresa Bonner

Set in Granjon by Keystone Typesetting, Inc.

Printed and bound by Thomson-Shore, Inc.

Library of Congress Cataloging-in-Publication Data

McGreevy, Patrick Vincent.

Imagining Niagara : the meaning and making of Niagara Falls /
Patrick V. McGreevy.

p.   cm.

Includes bibliographical references and index.

ISBN 0–87023–916–3 (alk. paper)

1. Niagara Falls (N.Y. and Ont.)   2. Niagara Falls Region (N.Y.
and Ont.)   I. Title.

F127.N8M43   1994

971.3′39—dc20   93–35720
                                                              CIP

British Library Cataloguing in Publication data are available.

This book is published with the support and cooperation of the
University of Massachusetts at Boston.

Several chapters in this book are revised versions of earlier, shorter articles:
chapter 2 appeared first as "Niagara as Jerusalem" in *Landscape* 27, no. 3 (1985):
26–32; chapter 3 appeared first as "Reading the Texts of Niagara Falls:
The Metaphor of Death" in *Writing Worlds: Discourse, Text & Metaphor in the
Representation of Landscape,* ed. James Duncan and Trevor Barnes (London:
Routledge, 1992): 50–72; and chapter five appeared as "Imagining the Future
at Niagara Falls" in *Annals of the Association of American Geographers* 77, no. 1
(1987): 48–62.

Buck Rogers ® material © 1929–1967, 1969 by The Dille Family Trust
and reprinted by permission of the Trust.

For
Helen and her father

CONTENTS

ILLUSTRATIONS

PREFACE

In the winter of 1973, I was working the midnight shift at one of the many factories that line the American shore of the Niagara River just above the falls. A group of my coworkers would occasionally take a drive during our 4 A.M. "lunch" break and return telling stories of their encounters with prostitutes and other "creatures" of the deep urban night. Eventually, I decided to venture out, but alone. Driving along deserted Buffalo Avenue through a string of irrelevant traffic lights, I felt a sudden impulse to go to the falls. I parked near the foot of Falls Street and walked out toward Prospect Point. When the lights of the city faded behind me, I could see nothing through the black, moonless night. But soon I became aware of a sound that gripped me: the seething, relentless rush of the river. Was it wise, I wondered, to leave the lighted city streets in this particular direction? My pace grew cautious. Then, through the trees, I glimpsed the sinuous black mass of the river, rolling out into the darkness: it seemed almost unearthly. I was fixed with awe. A light suddenly shone from behind me, and a human voice warned: "Don't do it!" It was a policeman, performing his job of guarding the boundary between darkness and light. Niagara Falls, he informed me, was "closed."

Many years later I learned that for an enormous number of people, a visit to Niagara has offered the possibility of transcending the ordinary—a powerful attraction for those whose more basic human needs have been secured. But this impulse to cross thresholds and experience what is beyond can also threaten stability. It is something that societies need to contain. This, to some extent, has been the cultural function of Niagara Falls: a place beyond ordinary places, it seems to demand a boundary—and police.

The physical landscape surrounding the cataract bears evidence of how, time and again, the boundary has failed to contain the seemingly exhaustless yearning for the extraordinary—and a portion of the "ordinary" world has therein been transformed. But the countervailing yearning for stability has inspired a largely successful movement to totally control the falls for human purposes. In the process, ironically, the very notion of a distinction, a boundary, between these two yearnings was the first casualty. The record of how individuals have experienced Niagara Falls, I believe, holds the key to understanding what has happened here. Exploring these issues is the task of this volume.

I wish to express my gratitude to Yi-Fu Tuan, Roger Miller, George Seibel, Donald Loker, Eliza McClennen, and Paul Wright, who have all helped me with this project in different ways. Several institutions have graciously given me access to rare materials; among them are the Buffalo and Erie County Historical Society, the Rochester Historical Society, the Niagara Falls (New York) Public Library, the Niagara Falls (Ontario) Public Library, and the Brock University Library. I owe a special debt of gratitude to Rev. Francis Schimscheiner, Mike Woldenberg, and again to Yi-Fu Tuan, a few of my teachers who not only profess their own deepest interests, but have encouraged me to do the same. Finally, I offer thanks to those who have sustained me in more personal ways: you know who you are.

IMAGINING
NIAGARA

IMAGINING NIAGARA

*N*iagara Falls is a strange place. People come by the millions to gaze at a small piece of natural landscape. Many no doubt are surprised to find this famous bit of nature embedded within a substantial city that straddles the border between Ontario and New York. Even more curious than Niagara's urban setting is the nature of that setting. Chemical industries, particularly on the American side, have created a gritty industrial landscape, a scene of environmental devastation made infamous by the Love Canal disaster. We are moved to ask how this could happen to a place idealized in the nineteenth century as the essence of natural sublimity. Another puzzling feature of this urban landscape is the unusual concentration of horror museums and similar carnival-like attractions that give Niagara Falls the atmosphere of a permanent side show. Since the early nineteenth century, a cir-cuslike atmosphere has continually prevailed here. In the center ring, an endless gallery of daredevils and tightrope walkers have sought acclaim by challenging the unruly river.

Perhaps H. G. Wells had some of these things in mind when he commented after a 1906 visit: "The real interest of Niagara for me was not in the waterfall but in the human accumulations around it."[1] What is peculiar is not only the *things* that accumulate in Niagara's landscape, but also the *people* who gather there—for example, the pilgrims who have journeyed to Niagara for religious reasons. The Catholic Church recognized these travelers in 1861 when it consecrated Niagara Falls a "pilgrim shrine," granting it the same official status as Jerusalem or Rome.[2] Then there are the thousands of honeymooners who come each year to celebrate their marriages. And finally, there are the many less-publicized visitors who come to Niagara to take their own lives.

All of this may arouse little curiosity among North Americans, but to a more distant observer—perhaps an anthropologist from another planet, if there were such a thing—the "human accumulations" at Niagara Falls might seem extraordinary indeed. To a cultural geographer the simple question is: Why here? Or to put it in slightly different terms: What do these human accumulations have to do with the waterfall itself? This book begins to answer this question, first, by examining the meanings people have ascribed to Niagara Falls, and then by seeking connections between these meanings and the puzzling accumulations. When we try to comprehend meanings, there is no ultimate theoretical bedrock on which to stand; we are thrown back on our own fragile ability to understand human creations because we, too, are human.[3] As Clifford Geertz puts it, "every serious cultural analysis starts from a sheer beginning."[4]

At Niagara Falls, there is no lack of evidence with which to begin. Over the last 350 years, people have articulated the meanings they have gleaned from the falls through nearly every medium of communication. There are literally millions of graphic images of Niagara, including etchings, paintings, and photographs. And there are thousands of written works that deal with Niagara Falls: travelers' descriptions, poems, plays, novels, and film scripts. One cannot help but be struck by the sheer amount of human attention the falls has attracted. For a great many North Americans and Europeans, Niagara has held a powerful fascination, an appeal to imagination. This, it seems, is the heart of the matter. But what exactly is the attraction?

My approach in this study was to look directly at how people have imagined Niagara Falls and determine what meanings they have attributed to the place. I found that a number of themes appear again and again in the literature and imagery of Niagara Falls. This book explores four of these themes that I believe are most crucial to understanding Niagara's appeal to the human imagination. Rather than systematically attempting to account for such things as honeymooning and chemical industries—the location of which clearly must be understood as multicausal— I more modestly try to draw connections between the meanings attributed to Niagara Falls and the various accumulations. Whereas a thematic exploration of Niagara's appeal cannot exhaustively explain all the accumulations, it can at least allow us to understand why, in terms of human imagination, Niagara is an appropriate setting for such things as honeymoons and chemical industries, circuses and suicides. The book's goals, in short, are interpretive and suggestive.

The four themes I examine in detail are quite distinct, yet each appeals to imagination in a similar way. The first is the geographic remoteness of Niagara Falls. Although Niagara was well known in Europe as early as the seventeenth century, it remained inaccessible to ordinary travelers until the completion of the Erie Canal in 1825. During this long period, there developed an image of the falls as an overwhelming spectacle. Niagara was a thing that could only be imagined, and Europeans imagined it as a fabulous place that had no parallel in their own world. They imbued it with all of the exotic possibilities attributed to the New World in general. Although Niagara's image blossomed in a cultural atmosphere of growing appreciation for the wild and powerful in nature, an important part of its early appeal was its isolation deep in the North American forest. The ideal Niagara Falls, many later visitors agreed, was experienced only by the early explorers who had seen the cataract uncontaminated by any human accumulations. "Blessed were the wanderers of old," wrote Nathaniel Hawthorne in 1834, "who heard its deep roar, sounding through the woods, as the summons to an unknown wonder, and approached its awful brink, in all the freshness of native feeling."[5] When travel finally became easier in the early nineteenth century, most visitors were those who had spent years imagining the falls from afar. For them, Niagara functioned as a remote goal beyond the known world. Many of these travelers called the journey a pilgrimage, and like their medieval predecessors, they thought of their destination as a place that transcended the limits of the ordinary world.

A second important focus, one that often appeared in the poetry and travelers' accounts of Niagara Falls, is the theme of death. The danger of death, of course, has always been real at Niagara. The fascination with this danger has led many writers to explore their ideas of death through elaborate symbolic interpretations of Niagara's landscape. One nineteenth-century poet, for instance, described the brink of the falls as "that thin line / That separates eternity from time."[6] At Niagara, many have been moved to speculate on the horrors and wonders that lie across that line. The world beyond death's opaque doors aroused their curiosity. Like a legendary waterfall in the heart of the colonial American wilderness, death opened into a world whose features could only be painted by the imagination.

A third emphasis in the literature and imagery of Niagara Falls is, not surprisingly, the subject of nature. Many have described the falls as an embodiment or symbol of nature, but the meanings they have deciphered in that symbol are diverse and complex. One can discern a fundamental similarity between nature and the themes of remoteness and death. At Niagara Falls, nature nearly always has been depicted as a boundless realm or power opposed to or beyond the world of human control. Some visitors have also identified nature with elements within the individual—such as the passions—that are not entirely under conscious control. In either case, the fascination with nature at Niagara has depended on the perception of a boundary between nature and the human world—a boundary that encircles and limits the human world, but leaves nature undefined and therefore open to the speculations and reveries of the human imagination.

The fourth important thematic focus is the future. Here we witness Niagara's grip on the imaginations not only of travelers and writers but also of engineers and entrepreneurs, many of whom, in the late nineteenth century, envisioned the fall's industrial and economic potential as limitless. They imagined a colossal, utopian future that would inevitably result from the relentless human drive to subdue and transform nature. At roughly the same time, however, there appeared several decidedly dystopian fictional visions of Niagara's future.

Each of these four themes evolved more or less independently, and indeed this book will examine them in four separate chapters. In one important sense, however, the themes are related: each presents a realm that contrasts with the ordinary here-and-now of daily life. Niagara's visitors are fascinated with these realms because they seem to offer the possibility of transcending the laws and limits of ordinary experience. The utter indeterminacy of these four realms encourages a certain exercise in imagination whereby a visit to Niagara Falls may stimulate an encounter with otherness. The encounter often turns out to be, in some manner, reflexive—an encounter with oneself. But it is the promise of the encounter, its imaginative appeal, that is central to Niagara's great attractiveness.

To the late-twentieth-century reader, these statements may appear far-fetched. It is probable that few of those who visit Niagara today regard their journey as a pilgrimage or a quest. It may therefore be difficult for us to appreciate the extent to which Niagara Falls stirred the imaginations of our predecessors. Indeed, the particular fascination with remote realms such as those represented by the four themes has often been associated with the nineteenth century and the culture of romanticism. Before I examine the historical dimension of this fascination, I will outline the chronology of Niagara's growth as a travel destination. This will help to clarify the relation of Niagara's literature to its wider cultural context.

The first noteworthy written description of Niagara Falls was published in France in 1683.[7] From then until the fall of Quebec in 1759, a mere trickle of visitors made the tortuous journey to Niagara. United Empire Loyalists began to settle on the west bank of the Niagara River during the Revolutionary War, and by the War of 1812, small communities had sprung up on the

Imagining Niagara

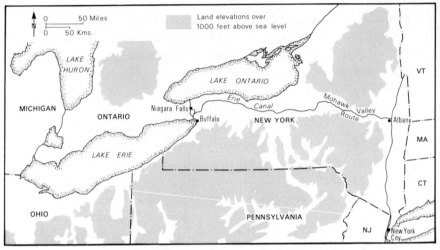

1. The Mohawk Valley provided a near sea-level route through the Appalachians, first successfully exploited by the Erie Canal.

American side. Only after this war, when the frontier of settlement approached the Niagara frontier, did travelers begin to arrive in any number with the express purpose of viewing the falls. With the opening of the Erie Canal, which exploited the gap in the Appalachians formed by the Mohawk Valley (figure 1), the thin stream of travelers increased to a torrent. And when the railroad reached Niagara from the seaboard in 1842, the torrent swelled to a flood. Thus began the heyday of Niagara Falls, its *belle epoque.* Between the War of 1812 and the Civil War, Niagara attracted the literary, artistic, and educated traveler. Out of the 187 nineteenth-century travelers' books we know of that describe Niagara, 139 originated in the half-century between 1810 and 1860.[8]

John Sears points out in his recent study of nineteenth-century American tourism that pleasure travel, although well established in Europe by the 1770s, did not commence with vigor in the United States until the 1820s.[9] Transportation improvements and the growth of a prosperous urban middle class were prerequisites to the creation of an American Grand Tour, which invariably included the Hudson River, the Erie Canal, and Niagara

Falls. The natural landscape took on a particular importance to America's cultural leaders at the time. Lacking the storied and long-humanized landscapes of England or France, the falls gave Americans a glimpse of a destiny of promise and grandeur. Indeed, Elizabeth McKinsey argues convincingly that Niagara served briefly as a nationalistic icon.[10] Throughout the nineteenth century, the nation's greatest writers and painters came to the falls to see what meanings they could discern amid its plunging waters. It is important to note, however, that its appeal was truly international: thousands of Europeans made the same pilgrimage to Niagara during this period. Like the image of America itself, the image of Niagara Falls was not confined to American imaginations alone.

Beginning in the 1820s, the landscape around Niagara Falls was gradually altered to accommodate the influx of visitors. Stairways, paths, and footbridges eased the visitor's approach to the cataract, and a stone tower provided panoramic views. Hotels, museums, peddlers, and numerous other accoutrements of the resort industry appeared on both banks.

After the Civil War, Niagara was no longer an exclusive retreat for the elite. A railroad journey to the great cataract was now within the means of many among the swelling middle class. In the early twentieth century, the automobile further democratized and diversified Niagara tourism. Ironically, as the falls grew less and less fashionable, it drew more and more visitors. Today's visitors form an annual horde estimated as high as 15 million.[11]

Elizabeth McKinsey suggests that, after the Civil War, Niagara was less and less the subject of good art, whether literary or graphic. Yet this transition was, in many ways, not nearly so striking as the one that took place in the early twentieth century. Major hydroelectric projects at the turn-of-the-century had for the first time palpably subdued Niagara's wild energy: humans could never again think of the cataract in the same way. As an indication of its attenuated power, in 1901, a middle-aged woman completed the first successful barrel trip over the falls.[12]

Visiting Niagara took on a different meaning after this period. Throughout the nineteenth century, writers, painters, even scientists felt obliged to come to Niagara and record their reactions to the sight. Even after the Civil War, people like Walt Whitman, William Dean Howells, Henry James, and H. G. Wells were drawn to the falls. What distinguishes these early visitors from those who came later is that a great number of them felt compelled to craft a personal response to the falls, which usually took a written form. It was common for nineteenth-century travelers to keep a journal, and because visiting Niagara was an important occasion in their lives, they often poured their thoughts and emotions onto the written page. In many cases the result was poetry or fiction. The abundant documents of these nineteenth-century visitors provide an intimate picture of how they experienced Niagara Falls—the trains of thought and fancy that the sight engendered. It is unfortunate that comparable evidence is so scarce for the twentieth century. The age of automobile travel apparently does not inspire an impulse toward introspection; only the camera remains to document the journey.

Thus, the scholar interested in the meanings people have attributed to Niagara Falls will find that the bulk of the evidence comes from the nineteenth century. This present investigation relies more upon written than pictorial evidence. One reason I have taken this approach is that most scholarly work on Niagara Falls to date has focused on and adequately documented Niagara's changing aesthetic appeal, primarily as it has been revealed through paintings.[13] Another reason is that, for the kind of interpretative framework employed here—one that attempts to draw connections between ideas, images, and meanings on the one hand, and landscape and social customs on the other—the written word is simply a richer and more articulate source. In a poem or travel journal entry, a writer can often be very explicit about the meaning of the scene and the ideas it seems to inspire. Writing is also a more democratic medium, at least in the sense that, before the advent of inexpensive twentieth-century photography, more of Niagara's visitors wrote descriptions than made graphic renderings in drawings or paintings. This does not mean that the written descriptions of Niagara Falls are somehow more important than the graphic ones, but simply that they are more useful for the purpose at hand.

The literature that this book scrutinizes in relation to the four themes is, like the Niagara literature in general, predominantly nineteenth-century in origin, with a slightly greater antebellum component. The one deviation from this is the literature pertaining to the final theme, the future, which is most in evidence at the end of the nineteenth and in the very early years of the twentieth century.

One might object that to understand the accumulations now visible at Niagara Falls, one ought to focus on more current evidence. But even if quality twentieth-century evidence were available, it would not be, for our purposes, as informative as that of the nineteenth century. Although Niagara has continued to change in many ways, most of the changes have been of degree rather than of quality—a product whose seeds were planted much earlier. The honeymoons, the suicides, the horror museums, and the industrial landscape were all well established before 1900. By that time, Niagara Falls had received as it were, a formative stamp. Nearly every kind of human accumulation that now seems curious at Niagara either began or had its roots in that earlier period. For an investigation that seeks to understand the presence of these accumulations, the nineteenth century is clearly central.

Looking at the broad historical and cultural context in which the phenomenon of Niagara Falls blossomed, we must remember that, before the eighteenth century, few saw value in wild, unhumanized parts of the natural world. Oceans, mountains, and cataracts were generally despised and feared. There was, of course, a long-standing appreciation of nature in its pastoral aspect, but this rested on nature's congeniality to, rather than its distance from, human life. Marjorie Hope Nicolson, in her study of English perceptions of the Alps,[14] found that travelers as late as the seventeenth century described mountains as the haunts of witches and as warts disfiguring the earth's surface. By the end of the eighteenth century, however, mountains were perceived as enchanted, awe-inspiring, and even sacred.

Nicolson argues that the roots of this transformation lay in the new picture of the cosmos elaborated by Copernicus, Kepler, and Galileo. Their crucial discovery was that the universe was neither static nor bounded. "In contemplating Space as in contemplating

God," she writes, "the soul of man was elated; released from finite limitations, it stretched its wings and took off into a vast universe of which there was no end, to seek the inexhaustible Good, and experienced triumph rather than despair because its quest must always remain unfinished." In this way, traditional religious sentiments of awe and delight were transferred to the created universe: "Awe, compounded of mingled terror and exaltation, once reserved for God, passed over in the seventeenth century first to an expanded cosmos, then from the macrocosm to the greatest objects of the geocosm."[15] In this broad sense, then, the attractiveness of places like Niagara Falls is a phenomenon of the modern Western world. Whether or not scientific conceptions were themselves as crucial as Nicolson suggests, clearly a refocusing of traditional religious sentiments was a prerequisite for the sort of enthusiasm nineteenth-century visitors showed toward Niagara Falls.

New developments in aesthetic thinking also contributed to Niagara's growing appeal. Early visitors were baffled by the combination of rapture and terror Niagara Falls seemed to inspire, but by the start of the nineteenth century, travelers had learned to relish such experiences and name them "sublime."[16] The word "sublime" entered the European vocabulary in the late seventeenth century when the work of the Greek rhetorician, Longinus, was rediscovered.[17] Longinus had considered the sublime a matter of rhetorical style, and this emphasis carried over into late seventeenth- and early eighteenth-century uses of the word. The sublime orator irresistibly convinces because of his ability to transport his audience. Gradually this stress on the power of artful words was replaced by a view of the sublime as a psychological response to sublime objects. Edmund Burke completed this transformation when he located the power to transport the mind in vast or frightening natural objects. Burke's treatise on the sublime (1757) was widely read well into the nineteenth century.[18] In Burke's view, a waterfall, volcano, or storm that inspired terror could only be sublime if the actual danger was at a distance. Near the end of the eighteenth century, Immanuel Kant argued that the source of the sublime was not the natural object itself but human nature. The natural sublime was a state of mind awakened by what was frightening and apparently unlimited in nature, and which ultimately led to an exalting realization of the viewer's own deepest powers. The idea of the natural sublime helped to clarify and, in some measure, encourage the growing taste for wild scenery. By the early nineteenth century, the theory had become so generally accepted that it provided both a justification for visitors' reactions and a vocabulary with which to express them.

When nineteenth-century visitors described Niagara Falls, they often made reference to my themes of geographical remoteness, death, nature, and the future. They seemed intent on leaving their ordinary worlds behind, as if the journey were a purposeful approach to a threshold, culminating in a glimpse of something literally extraordinary. In this sense, Niagara Falls appears to have functioned as a device for reverie—a screen on which nineteenth-century Europeans and Americans could project their personal explorations of certain collective preoccupations. For many visitors, Niagara Falls became not only a stimulus for reflection but also a metaphor for death, nature, or the future. Because each of these realms was, again, characterized by its remoteness from ordinary experience—its epistemological opacity—each also served as a tableau by which visitors could explore, in a somewhat more focused manner, important preoccupations of their age. Because the meanings of death, nature, and the future, along with related issues pertaining to technology and religion, were themselves topics of much interest and discussion in the nineteenth century, there is in the Niagara literature an intertextual relation to this larger discussion. Indeed, what we have at Niagara might be characterized as a dialogue on these themes, albeit a largely unself-conscious one.[19] The Niagara literature offers glimpses of nineteenth-century soul-searching and speculation that are symptomatic of a more general cultural turmoil.

In its more immediate cultural context, the Niagara literature is intimately connected with romanticism. The ascendancy of romanticism in the first half of the nineteenth century coincides temporally with Niagara's own ascendancy; more important, many of the central concerns of the romantics are also voiced in the Niagara literature. "The primary experience that identifies a romantic," writes Michael Hoffman, "is his inevitable consciousness of the void beneath the conventional structures of 'reality'."[20] Thus, a figure like Thoreau could muster no enthusiasm "to live in this restless, nervous, bustling, trivial Nineteenth Century."[21] To the romantics, everyday life—particularly in its public aspects—held little of value. "It is a sign of our times," wrote Emerson, "that many intelligent and religious persons withdraw themselves from the common labors and competitions of the market and the caucus."[22] This, of course, was not solely an American perception; Wordsworth's familiar sonnet begins: "The world is too much with us; late and soon / Getting and spending, we lay waste our powers."

But if the world close at hand had become petty and banal, the romantics could imagine a world beyond the here and now that was burdened with none of these limitations. Hence, Melville's Ishmael is "tormented by an everlasting itch for things remote."[23] Indeed, a number of scholars have commented on the romantics' fascination with remoteness of various forms.[24] For F. L. Lucas, romantic subject matter concerns

> always "la princesse lointaine," the blue of distance. For remoteness is a feeling associated with dreams; and again, remoteness makes it easier to dream—there is less danger of colliding with a brute fact. It may be remoteness in time. . . . Or it may be remoteness in space. . . . Or, again, it may be that other remoteness of undiscovered countries of the mind. "Who," says Fuller, "hath sailed about the world of his own heart, sounded each creek, surveyed each corner, but that there still remains much *terra incognita* in himself?"[25]

The lure of the remote held an unprecedented power during the age of Romanticism, but it is a lure that certainly transcends that age. The fascination with distant lands, for instance, had been growing since before the Renaissance. Nevertheless, a good case can be made that there is something new about the romantic's view of the remote. W. H. Auden presents such an argument by drawing a contrast between the legend of Ulysses' last voyage as it appeared in Dante's medieval treatment and in Tennyson's version. Dante placed Ulysses in hell for venturing forth a second time from Ithaca, while Tennyson idealized Ulysses' insatiable curiosity. It was not the attraction to remote lands that was new, but rather how one's yielding to that attraction was evaluated. To the author of the *Inferno,* venturing forth was a sin, while to Tennyson and the romantics it had become, in Auden's words, "the desire of every man of sensibility and honor."[26]

Both the growing attractiveness of Niagara Falls and the emergence of romanticism must be understood in relation to certain contemporaneous material and social developments. The physical relation between humans and the natural world was rapidly changing, and by the eighteenth century, as Clarence Glacken points out, the increasing human ability to manipulate and control the natural environment had crystallized the separation between humans and nature. This realization, in turn, helped to erode the teleological view that nature had been designed solely for human habitation. If nature was more than a backdrop for human activity, it might contain beauties and secrets in its own right.[27]

The vigorous onset of industrial capitalism by the first half of the nineteenth century brought important technological, geographical, and social changes. The steam engine, the railroad, and the products spewing out of factories quickened the pace at which the natural environment was being subdued. In both Western Europe and North America, the new economic system fostered a rapid and unprecedented urbanization. The growing middle class found itself at a great "distance from nature,"[28] and considering the well-documented unpleasantness of the immediate urban environment, it is not surprising that many from this class should begin to idealize what had become remote: the least humanized parts of nature.

For the first time, the industrial system severed the household from the world of productive work.[29] Many found the competitive public realm of industry, commerce, and government mean-spirited, trivial, and alienating.[30] People like Thoreau and Emerson, although benefiting materially from the new economic order, reacted adversely to the banality of daily life in the nineteenth century and ascribed value to realms distant from that life in time, space, or character. The bourgeois way of life, argues Georg Lukacs, consists of "a renunciation of all brilliance in life so that all the brilliance, all the splendor may be transferred elsewhere."[31] Surely, some of these discontents helped to fuel the fascination not only with Niagara Falls, but also with death, nature, and the future.

Thematically considered, the literature of Niagara Falls might best be compared to a great romantic novel such as *Moby Dick*.[32] Although the novel clearly attempts a unity of design that the body of Niagara literature lacks, each engages important nineteenth-century concerns. Among the most basic of these was the meaning of nature in light of new human abilities and sensibilities. Whereas this Promethean theme "belongs to no single time or place," Leo Marx argues, it could have "a particular relevance to an age suddenly aware that machines were making life over new."[33] Both Niagara Falls and Moby Dick are pictured as singular, sublime natural objects, the one isolated in the interior wilderness, the other lurking in the "everlasting terra incognita" (305) of the sea. Each is freighted with layers of symbolic meaning. Each is associated with death, "a speechlessly quick chaotic bundling of a man into Eternity" (49). Indeed, it is by the "whiteness" of the whale, by its opacity, "by its indefiniteness [that] it shadows forth the heartless voids and immensities of the universe" (218). Moby Dick is a "phantom that, some time or other, swims before all human hearts" who pursue "those far mysteries we dream of" (264).

To think about the geographically remote and about death, nature, and the future, is to consider the temporal and physical limits of human life. Many of Niagara's visitors have engaged in imagining and speculating about what lies beyond those limits. Although their curiosity, their quest to penetrate those barriers, could rarely match Ahab's in intensity, these visitors nevertheless shared something of the desire he expresses when he says: "All visible objects are but pasteboard masks. . . . How can the prisoner reach outside except by thrusting through the wall? To me, the white whale is that wall, shoved near to me" (184). The story of Niagara Falls ends differently from Melville's tale: Ahab's ship, with its whale-consuming "artificial fire" (464), is swallowed by the sea; but at Niagara Falls, a group of nineteenth-century developers, with eyes fixed on a limitless future, began the process that ultimately subdued the cataract entirely, transmuting its plunging water into the "artificial fire" of hydroelectric power. This leviathan did not escape: only its mask survives.

THE DISTANT NIAGARA

*W*hen word of Niagara Falls first reached Europe, the falls almost immediately took on the proportions of myth. Niagara's supreme isolation allowed seventeenth-century Europeans to imagine it as a fabulous, overwhelming place, a place with no parallel in their own world. These initial perceptions proved to be remarkably persistent, so much so that until the end of the nineteenth century, people continued to measure the falls, not against other grand objects, not against what they had seen, but against what they could imagine. Niagara was a place set apart; it was a goal of travelers, a place outside the sphere of normal life. As an ideal, such a place offers to the traveler the hope of escaping the confines of daily life and entering a world full of possibilities.

This chapter focuses on how Niagara Falls has been viewed through the veil of distance. The first section examines the development of a European fascination with faraway lands, which helped to make the image of Niagara's otherworldly magnificence believable. The second section traces how, from a distance, this image began to develop, how it unfolded, and how it persisted long after the cataract had ceased to be remote. The final section focuses on a recurrent image often expressed in the nineteenth century: many travelers described the journey to Niagara as a pilgrimage. Like medieval Christian pilgrims, these travelers idealized their distant goal, and they hoped to have something like a transcendent experience when they reached that goal. They aspired, through their ritual journey, to be released—if only temporarily—from the limitations of a commonplace world. The similarities between these nineteenth-century travelers and pilgrims will suggest interpretations of two intriguing facets of Niagara Falls that have endured into our century: Niagara's circus atmosphere and its role as a honeymoon resort.

The first reports of Niagara Falls reached Europe via French missionaries and explorers around 1670. This was an opportune time, because, as Marjorie Hope Nicolson and others have suggested, Europeans at this time had begun to develop a new attitude about the world that allowed them to picture a remote natural phenomenon as extremely attractive. The traditional world of the Middle Ages had been very restrictive. The repeating calendar of feasts and festivals had enclosed the individual in a cycle from which there was no escape. Yi-Fu Tuan describes the medieval conception of the cosmos as vertical, for it was the vertical dimension that signified transcendence. The individual consequently played "two roles, the social-profane and the mythical-sacred, the one bound to time, the other transcending it."[1] Between 1500 and 1700, a new conception of the world emerged. The cyclical time of the medieval calendar were exchanged for a linear view of time, and a new fascination with depth and spacious landscapes in painting signaled the beginning of what Tuan calls the "axial transformation" to a horizontal world view.[2] Europeans began to look to the distant horizon and the future with intense anticipation. With characteristic sweep, Lewis Mumford has suggested that the transition from a medieval to a modern consciousness meant that

> people were no longer content to remain within their walls:
> walls of class, walls of occupation, walls of fixed duties and
> obligations, walls of cities and territories. They had a sense

that a new world lay outside their self-imposed boundaries: space summoned them. . . . By degrees, Western man lost his respect for boundaries: the unknown, the untried, the unbounded began to tempt his imagination. . . .[3]

This attitude expressed itself geographically in a fascination with the world outside of Europe, a fascination that both propelled and fed upon the process of discovery.

The fascination with remote lands was not entirely new. The Dutch historian Henri Baudet has traced its roots to the very origin of Western civilization. These images of unknown lands, he argues, are derived from "an inner urge that does not stem from objective facts—gold, silver, spices, etc.—but from nostalgia for the deep, the ideal, the ultimate harmony still cherished as the real purpose of creation."[4] The human condition in Western civilization, from both its Greek and its Judeo-Christian roots, is understood as originating in a fall from an ideal state. It is out of a kind of Promethean guilt, then, in Baudet's view, that the European sees those lands untouched by Western civilization as paradisaical, unfallen. But Baudet fails to adequately point out a paradox here. Adam's act of defiance is a gamble of one not completely satisfied with Paradise; like Prometheus's act, it is an attempt to procure for mankind something of the divine. The attraction to remote lands shares this paradox: it is not only prelapsarian comfort that is imagined but also a new and higher kind of life. The paradox is that remote lands can appeal to both of these urges—for comfort and for intensity of life.

More relevant to the early perceptions of Niagara Falls are the speculations of medieval Europeans about what lay beyond the boundaries of their world. Because they lacked an attitude that favored exploration, they did little more than speculate. Yet these speculations created an image of the world outside of Europe that proved remarkably durable and that helped to spur the dynamics of discovery.

The American geographer John Kirtland Wright, who investigated the medieval image of the world beyond Europe at some length, described the geographical knowledge that the Middle Ages bequeathed to the early modern world as comprised within two concentric circles: a very broad outer circle, which includes all those lands of which knowledge had been derived at second hand through literary sources; and a smaller inner circle including those lands which were known at first hand through actual travel.

The outer circle took in to the east the land of Seres, or China, and the lost Atlantis to the west; and to the south the Mons Climax of Ptolemy and the mysterious upper reaches of the Nile. Nearly all that lies between the two was a vague region of fancy and fable. . . .[5]

Knowledge of what lay beyond the inner circle was based upon "literary sources"—chiefly the Bible—and upon "fancy and fable." According to these sources, the contents of this outer region could be characterized as wholly unlike the contents of the inner circle. Out there both the horrible and the beautiful existed in greater intensity than in the known world.

Among the more terrifying things one might encounter by venturing beyond the rim of the known world were enormous whirlpools that sucked in ships that came too near. One could also expect to see giants, monsters, and "mouths of Hell." But perhaps the most dreaded of all things which Europeans imagined to lie outside of Europe were the lands of the fierce tribes of Gog and Magog—in most accounts, located somewhere in Asia, where they were reportedly confined behind huge walls. According to the Book of Revelation, Satan would gather these tribes together when he was released at the end of time and destroy the world.[6]

The people of the Middle Ages also imagined wonderful things beyond the borders of the European world. One of the most universal beliefs was that Paradise or the Garden of Eden still existed somewhere on earth. In many maps of the period, paradise appeared at the easternmost edge of the world following the Genesis account: "And the Lord God planted a garden eastward in Eden."[7] Some believed that it lay to the north, while others, in accordance with the legend of St. Brandan, placed it in the west. The accounts generally agreed that the garden was inaccessible. Many authors surrounded it with mountains, deserts, or flames, while others placed it on an island in the ocean or upon lands beyond the ocean.[8]

Another widespread belief was that a powerful Christian king, Prester John, ruled a vast domain of seventy-two kingdoms in the heart of Asia. The legends described Prester John's kingdom as almost unlimited in size and wealth. It contained rivers that offered forth large quantities of gold and gems at regular intervals and a spring that gave eternal youth to all who bathed in it. This was only one of the many medieval legends concerning a Fountain of Youth.[9]

Prester John's rivers of gold and gems were also part of a larger narrative. Throughout the Middle Ages, Europeans imagined lands of fabulous riches somewhere to the east. Several medieval mapmakers, for example, located the biblical land of Ophir in India. Ophir had long been associated with gold and had reportedly supplied great quantities of the precious metal to Solomon.[10] Isidore of Seville, the first of the great encyclopedists who attempted to compile the remnants of classical geographical knowledge, claimed that the islands of the Indian Ocean were teeming with precious metals where dragons and griffins served as guardians for entire mountains of gold. Arab sources that eventually made their way into Europe via Spain and mercantile centers such as Venice enhanced this picture. Moslem traders knew well that pepper, silk, jade, and porcelain came from the east, but the Arab astronomer Al-Battani preferred to repeat the inherited stories: "Upper Scythia, stretching from the Caspian Sea to the Seric Ocean [the China Sea] and southward to the Caucasus, includes much habitable land but also much that is sterile: gold and gems abound there, but men avoid them on account of the griffins."[11] The most renowned of Arab travelers was, of course, the legendary Sinbad. Among his adventures in India was a visit to a valley of diamonds which was guarded by large snakes.[12]

When Marco Polo published the story of his eastern travels at the end of the thirteenth century, he reconfirmed the image of oriental riches. Not only was the East a land of diamonds, rubies, and gold, but also of fabulous cities. The city of Kinsai, he estimated, was a hundred miles in circumference and contained 12,000 bridges.[13] Although the Orient was most often the locus of riches in early European lore, eventually other locales—particularly the West—took on the same meaning. According to Iberian folklore, for example, six bishops and an archbishop escaped westward across the Atlantic Ocean during the Moorish invasion of Spain and founded seven cities of gold.[14]

Medieval Europeans, we can agree, had a rather fantastic image of the unknown lands that surrounded them. They populated the unknown with wonders and horrors unlike anything seen in the known world. It is worth remembering, however, that when speculation contradicted the authority of tradition or Scripture, it was considered, in the words of St. Boniface, "perverse and iniquitous." Even late in the Middle Ages, such speculators were sometimes burned to death.[15]

When trust in authority finally began to wane and Europeans set out to see for themselves what was "out there," the medieval speculations did much to inspire them. Because it was Africa and the Near East that first captured the imaginations of Europeans, Prince Henry of Portugal initiated a vast effort to find the legendary kingdom of Prester John, which he believed was in Ethiopia.[16] Slowly, Europeans became more and more enticed by the western ocean. When a New World was found there, many believed that it must be a fabulous world. This sense of expectation had been conditioned by a long history of speculation and legend concerning the Ocean Sea to the west.

Howard Mumford Jones, in his study of European perceptions of the New World, has observed that "the belief in riches and perfection beyond the sunset is very old in Europe."[17] Greek dramatists spoke of a western paradise and Romans reported voyages to the Islands of the Blest, somewhere to the west of Spain. The Middle Ages contributed new stories of such western voyagers as St. Brandan and the Zeno brothers of Venice. These legends probably had little basis in fact, but as Jones points out, "the point is, surely, not whether somebody got to Greenland and the North American continent or learned vaguely about the glories of pre-Columbian Mexico, the point is the splendor, the wonder, the haunting riches at the edge of the world."[18] By the time of Columbus, Europeans perceived the Atlantic as an Ocean Sea speckled with strange islands, some wonderful, some terrifying, some holding great riches and some social or religious perfection. After the Portuguese failed to discover the earthly paradise in Africa, many Europeans turned to the west, believing that Eden must lie there. Columbus believed he had found it at the mouth of the Orinoco in South America. He was unable to mount an expedition to the source of the river where, as he put it, "I believe in my soul that the earthly paradise is situated."[19]

Following Columbus's voyages, old images of wealth and wonder inspired further discoveries. Ponce de Leon trekked through the swamps and lakes of Florida searching for the Fountain of Youth. An image of the fabled Seven Cities of Gold spurred Coronado, de Soto, and others to explore vast tracts of western North America. These legends obviously could not long endure in the face of vigorous exploration, but the general image of the New World proved much more lasting. Indeed, that world beyond the western sea became the logical location for perfection in such diverse works as Bacon's *New Atlantis,* More's *Utopia,* Shakespeare's *Tempest,* and Blake's *America: A Prophecy.* Jones argues that this image survived into the twentieth century in the idea of "an economy of abundance" and "in the dream of millions of emigrants that life is 'better' in the New World."[20] Certainly this image of a fabulous New World was still robust when word of Niagara Falls first reached Europe. Early modern Europeans were prepared to imagine the extraordinary in that distant land beyond the ocean.

An expedition led by Robert Cavelier, Sieur de La Salle, camped on the Upper Niagara River in 1669. Although the camp was less than five miles from the falls, neither La Salle nor any of his party went to see it. A Sulpitian missionary with the expedition, René de Brehant de Galinee, however, questioned the Seneca inhabitants of the region concerning the cataract. Using their knowledge, he was able to write a surprisingly accurate description. He concluded with the following comments:

Our desire to go to our little village called Ganastogue Sonon-
toua Outinaouatoua prevented our going to see that wonder,
which I regarded as so much the greater, as the River St.
Lawrence is one of the largest in the world. I leave you to
imagine if it is not a beautiful cascade, to see all the water in
this great river, which at its mouth is three leagues in width,
precipitate itself from a height of two hundred feet with a roar
that is heard not only from the place we were, ten or twelve
leagues distant, but actually from the other side of Lake
Ontario, opposite its mouth. . . .[21]

It is fitting to begin with Galinee's account not only because it
is the earliest detailed description of the falls, but also because it
suggests an image of Niagara that was to reverberate for at least
two centuries—the image of a waterfall whose nature lies beyond our powers of empirical observation, a waterfall we are left
to imagine. For 150 years after Galinee's account, Niagara remained inaccessible to all but a few, but his description and others
that followed quickly made Niagara Falls well known. During
this long period of inaccessibility, however, the readers of these
accounts, like Galinee himself, could only imagine a falls that
they could not see.

Louis Hennepin, the famous Recollect missionary, accompanied La Salle on his second expedition (1678–79) and published
several descriptions of Niagara Falls which were widely read in
Europe. He was probably the first white man actually to see the
falls.[22] Hennepin's first account (1683) is brief and factual.[23] He
was obviously impressed, but he elaborated on neither the scene
itself nor his reaction to it. Nineteen years after his visit, Hennepin published his final description of the falls. Through the veil
of time and distance, he now portrayed Niagara as a deeply
stirring sight: "When one stands near the Fall, and looks down
into this most dreadful Gulph, one is seized with Horror. . . ."
Like many others after him, he lamented the inadequacy of his
powers of description. Most interesting, perhaps, is his observation that the waters plunge "into the Gulph with all the violence
that can be imagin'd."[24] Here at the very beginning is the key
image of Niagara Falls as a thing commensurate with our power
to imagine, as something unconfined by the limits we associate

with everyday reality. Europeans, it seems, were eager to accept this image of Niagara, as the iconography of the falls illustrates. Hennepin published the first picture of Niagara Falls in 1697. Like his written accounts, it greatly exaggerated their height. Yet, despite the availability of more accurate views, Hennepin's picture remained the standard image of Niagara for over 100 years. It continued to inspire copies for 150 years,[25] copies that often further exaggerated Niagara's height.

The few who wrote first-hand descriptions in the eighteenth century often described the falls as limitless in one way or another, an observation that continued to appear throughout the nineteenth century. Some saw Niagara as timeless or eternal, others as infinitely powerful, and still others as bottomless.[26] The Swedish botanist Peter Kalm, who gave us the first English description of the falls in 1751, wrote:

> The French told me, they had often thrown whole great trees into the water above, to see them tumble down the Fall. They went down with surprising swiftness, but could never be seen afterwards; whence it was thought there was a bottomless deep or abyss just under the Fall.[27]

In moments of reverie, many later visitors have also pondered over the depth of the plunge. On the eve of the American Civil War, for example, Anthony Trollope—a British novelist of a decidedly realist cast—mused: "It is so far down—far as your imagination can sink it."[28] Here again is the notion that one requires imagination to comprehend Niagara. Those who knew it only from afar through the written and pictorial descriptions of others were not necessarily at a disadvantage in their comprehension.

Of the hundreds of nineteenth-century poems that Niagara inspired, the most widely acclaimed was written by a man who had never been to Niagara—a Connecticut newspaper editor named John C. Brainard. Although he had seen the falls only in his mind's eye, he was able to compose in the 1840s these most repeated of all lines on Niagara: "Deep calleth onto deep. And what are we / That hear the question of that voice sublime?"[29]

With the opening of the Erie Canal in 1825, many finally

found it possible to consider a trip to Niagara. Yet these travelers were in a situation much like that of the eighteenth-century Europeans. Whereas they had read descriptions and perhaps viewed pictures of Niagara, the journey itself could still probably be made only once in a lifetime, thus heightening expectations. Niagara was a place they had imagined at great length from a distance, but reality could disappoint. Consider the reaction of Mrs. A.B.M. Jameson, a British writer steeped in the romantic movement. She traveled to the falls in 1836:

> Well, I have seen these cataracts of Niagara which have thundered in my mind's ear ever since I can remember—which have been my childhood's thought, my youth's desire, since first my imagination was awakened to wonder and to wish. I have beheld them; I wish I had not! I wish they were still a thing to behold—a thing to be imagined, hoped and anticipated—something to live for—the reality has displaced from my mind an illusion far more magnificent than itself.[30]

Nathaniel Hawthorne came with similar expectations in 1834. He wrote: "I had come thither haunted with a vision of foam and fury and dizzy cliffs, and an ocean tumbling down out of the sky. . . . My mind struggled to adapt these false conceptions to the reality, and finding the effort vain, a wretched sense of disappointment weighed me down."[31] Through sustained effort at contemplation, Hawthorne was finally able to imagine himself alone with the cataract like the "wanderers of old."[32] He was able personally to transform his inflated image of Niagara and leave satisfied with the experience.

Nevertheless, many other nineteenth-century travelers found their preconceptions fulfilled at Niagara Falls. James Dixon, a Connecticut congressman who dabbled in poetry, offered these reflections after visiting the falls in 1848: "Who can grasp the Infinite? God has left, in all his dominions and works, space for imagination. Everything has its mystery,—nothing its limits. Niagara stands as a mystic creation, defying the admeasurements of the human intellect."[33] For visitors such as Dixon, distance was not necessary to make Niagara seem extraordinary, for even when face to face with the cataract, there was "space for imagination." It was as if the falls while proximate were still remote. The chapters that follow focus on three specific ways that nineteenth-century visitors found to experience Niagara as if it were, in a sense, still remote. But first, one additional characterization of Niagara Falls warrants attention because, like the first views of the falls from Europe, it involves an idealization from a distance.

The perception of Niagara Falls as a place where the extraordinary might be possible had begun in a period when the cataract was nearly inaccessible; it endured until much later among the many individuals who could anticipate an actual journey to the falls. It was a perception remarkably similar to the traditional view of the pilgrim's goal: a "center out there,"[34] where one could hope to transcend, at least temporarily, the boundaries of the routine world. When regular travel to Niagara became feasible, many writers began to recognize the similarity between Niagara and the religious pilgrim center. In 1839, the British visitor Thomas Grinfield offered this interpretation in his "Hymn on Niagara":

> And still the thunder of the eternal anthem,
> And still the column of ascending incense,
> Shall draw remotest pilgrims to thy worship,
> Shall hold them breathless in thy sovereign presence,
> And lost to all that they before had look'd on;
> Yea, conjur'd up by strong imagination,
> Shall sound in ears that never heard the music,
> Shall gleam in eyes that ne'er beheld the vision;
> Till the great globe, with all that it inherits,
> Shall vanish,—like that cloud of ceaseless incense,—
> In thunder,—like that falling world of water.[35]

Lines like these suggest that, as an ideal, the journey to Niagara could closely resemble a pilgrimage. The "remotest pilgrims" are drawn by "strong imagination" into a vision where this world and "all that it inherits" vanish "like that falling world of waters." This was the vision long anticipated from far away. The pilgrim's view of Niagara, like the explorer's view of the New World, was a view from a distance nurtured in imagination. Clearly, there are similarities between Niagara Falls and the religious pilgrim center, but what are the attributes of a pilgrim center, and how well do they fit Niagara Falls?

Nathaniel Hawthorne, who, as we saw, expected to find "an ocean tumbling down out of the sky," began his description of Niagara by confessing: "Never did a pilgrim approach Niagara with deeper enthusiasm than mine." Like Hawthorne, the devout pilgrims of the Middle Ages expected their goal to be fabulous. To their eyes, the pilgrim center—be it Rome, Jerusalem, Compostella, or Canterbury—was a place different in nature from the towns and villages they had come from. These pilgrims journeyed in anticipation toward a place where, they believed, a timeless world was connected to their own. The *Guide Du Pelerin* (Pilgrim's Guide) by the twelfth-century monk Aimery Picaud described the tomb of St. James at Compostella as a place palpably infused with the supernatural. The tomb, Picaud wrote, was "ceaseless honored by sweet, divine odors, embellished by the radiance of celestial torches and surrounded by the cares of attentive angels."[36] Pilgrimage promised the individual a glimpse or a simulation of eternity. As Donald Howard has pointed out, pilgrimage was a "metaphor for human life: life is a one-way passage to the Heavenly Jerusalem."[37] The goal of a pilgrimage was, ultimately, out of this world.

The anthropologist Victor Turner, who has examined the pilgrimage process in diverse cultures, argues that, in a social sense at least, the traditional pilgrim did step out of the ordinary world. Indeed, much of the appeal of pilgrimage even today is that it offers an opportunity to escape the conventions and routines of daily life. Turner cites this description of a pilgrimage:

> For three days and nights, the emotional tension and the religious atmosphere, together with the relaxation of certain moral restrictions, performed the psychosocial function of temporarily removing the participants from their preoccupation with small-group convention-ridden, routinized daily life and placing them into another context of existence—the activities and feelings of the larger community.[38]

The pilgrimage, in Turner's words, opposes "cosmopolitanism to local particularism." The traveling pilgrim "comes across markets and fairs, especially at the end of his quest, where the shrine is flanked by the bazaar and the fun fair. But all these things are more contractual, more associational, more volitional, more replete with the novel and the unexpected . . . than anything he has known at home."[39]

Undertaking a pilgrimage is a personal decision. Turner compares the pilgrimage to a quest in which "the hero or heroine goes on a long journey to find out who he or she really is outside structure."[40] Leaving the structured world of home, the pilgrim enters what Turner calls a liminal state. Turner's interest in liminal states began with his earlier ethnographical studies in Central Africa. During rites of passage such as circumcision rituals, he found that the initiates were temporarily removed from the structures of ordinary social life. The initiates became equals regardless of their previous relationships, and they often experienced a strong sense of brotherhood that seemed tied to neither blood nor locality. Turner argues that these characteristics are also present during pilgrimage.

The pilgrim enters a liminal state at the beginning of the journey, but it is the pilgrim center itself that represents the opposite pole to the structure of home life. Turner writes:

> A limen is, of course, literally a "threshold." A pilgrim center, from the standpoint of the believing actor, also represents a "threshold," a place and moment "in and out of time," and such an actor—as the evidence of many pilgrims of many religions attests—hopes to have there direct experience of the sacred, invisible, or supernatural order, either in the material aspect of a miraculous healing or in the immaterial aspect of inward transformation of spirit or personality.[41]

The pilgrim's quest for transcendent experience reaches its climax at the pilgrim center, which, for the believer, is a sacred place. Indeed, the pilgrim center is usually a site where, "according to believers, some manifestation of divine or supernatural power had occurred,"[42] as, for instance, in the modern examples of Fatima and Lourdes.

Nevertheless, some medieval pilgrims were not enthusiastic about the journey and perhaps expected little of their goal. The travelers in Chaucer's *Canterbury Tales,* for instance, seem to be little more than tourists. Moreover, as the Middle Ages waned, pilgrimages were often enforced as criminal sentences, and some pilgrims even became professionals, offering to perform proxy pilgrimages for a fee. Similarly, some people traveled to Niagara in the nineteenth century with no great sense of expectation or ceremony. However, in looking at pilgrims of both periods, it is appropriate to focus on those who were inspired by an ideal image of their goal, because this image gave the travel its allure and its special character.

The first long journey made solely to visit Niagara Falls—the first pilgrimage, we might say—was undertaken from Montreal in 1721 by four French officers, including the son of New France's governor.[43] For most of the eighteenth century, the falls remained cut off from the coast by the lands of the powerful Six Nations Confederacy, and visitors came only in a trickle. With the defeat of the Six Nations and the subsequent settlement of the area— first by United Empire Loyalists during the American Revolution and soon afterward by Yankees—came greater accessibility. By 1810, settlement was continuous from New York to the Niagara River.[44] By mid-century, the Erie Canal and the railroad made it possible for Niagara Falls to become, in the words of one English visitor, "the goal and object of western travel."[45] Of course, since that time, the numbers have continued to increase.

Turner's analysis of pilgrimage suggests that many of Niagara's visitors should be classified as tourists rather than pilgrims. Yet most tourists have something in common with pilgrims. They too leave behind the structured world of their ordinary lives: they are on vacation. Lukermann and Porter describe the utopian ideal that underlies the modern vacation, as it is promoted in the literature of tourism and as it is to some extent popularly believed: "Consider what a vacation is supposed to be. One escapes the real world to a setting, often isolated and idyllic, of peace and abundance. One's identity and class distinctions may be suspended as on other unreal or ritual occasions, such as Mardi Gras and masked balls."[46]

Although pilgrims and tourists have something essential in common, there is still a distinction to be made. They are perhaps best considered as endpoints of a continuum. The pages that follow are intended only to establish that a significant proportion of Niagara's visitors, particularly in the nineteenth century, thought and acted very much like pilgrims. To these travelers, Niagara Falls was a sacred place and their journey was a momentous quest.

Perhaps the clearest evidence that some of Niagara's visitors were no ordinary tourists is their stated motivation for making the journey. Consider, for example, the testimony of George Houghton, an editor and poet active in New York City's literary circles. He came to Niagara in 1882, "striving, by travail and tears," to grasp "life's deeper meaning." In a moment of despair, when his quest for an ultimate answer seemed doomed, he addressed the waterfall:

Faith in thee I have none! I lift spent eyes, and despairing,
Set my teeth in defiance. Fate, then, the father of all things!
I but a victim moth, to be snatched by a merciless current,
Dragged by cold eddies down, to be lost and forgotten forever!

Why then this pilgrimage here? God knows no willful self-
    seeking
Lent us this restless life; and no faint-heart or rebellion
Gives us this fear to lie down, and rest in the slumberous
    dreamland!
—Answer, if answer thou hast! Answer, Niagara, Answer![47]

Katherine Lee Bates, the Wellesley professor who wrote the lyrics to "America the Beautiful," ended her poem, "Song of Niagara" (1910), with a similar plea: "Is there no meaning in your ceaseless song, / No word of God in all your mighty throng / Of multitudinous thunders evermore?"[48]

Other travelers described the goal of the quest as an experience rather than an answer. Like religious pilgrims, they hoped to experience a moment of timelessness, of transcendence. They hoped to be transformed. Whether these travelers came to Niagara seeking an experience of transcendence or an answer to the riddle of life, they—like traditional pilgrims—thought of their destination as a sacred place.

On what grounds could a place with no explicit religious significance be considered sacred? Niagara had no sacred history. It had little human history. It was a natural place. Yet, by the eighteenth century, European attitudes toward such places had begun no change. God, after all, was responsible for the form of natural places. For many Europeans, it had become possible to see God's majesty in mountains, oceans, and cataracts. Some believed that God expressed himself at Niagara in a special way. Abraham Coles, like many of Niagara's nineteenth-century visitors, tried his hand at poetry, although he was more talented as a translator and most of his income derived from his Newark, New Jersey, medical practice. In his "Sabbath at Niagara" (1881), Coles wrote:

> O, let my heart exult,
> That here she may consult,
>   The Oracle Divine!
> That at Jerusalem, no more,
> Is fixed as heretofore
>   Jehovah's Shrine!
> That ancient ritual is past,
> That temple to the ground is cast,
> Those symbols and those semblances sublime,
>   Endured but for a time.
> Their everlasting prototypes, I ween,
> Their patterns on the Mount by Moses seen,
>   Were these, are here!
>   This much at least is clear;
> If, in th'immensity of space,
> God makes one spot his special dwelling-
> place,
>   That spot is this.[49]

There were two reasons to consider Niagara sacred: either it was an expression of nature or of God. The first view was based on the belief, which certainly reached its zenith in the nineteenth century, that nature itself was sacred. The second was explicitly religious but nevertheless related to the first, for a certain view of nature was required before a religious person could find a waterfall comparable to places hallowed by recognized sacred events or relics. In the minds of nineteenth-century travelers, the two views were sometimes complexly mingled, but for clarity we will consider the two separately.

Many deeply religious people were attracted to Niagara Falls in the nineteenth century. It was a worthy goal of pilgrimage, they believed, because God, in creating it, had revealed his majesty in an unparalleled way. To see Niagara was therefore to glimpse God's majesty, and perhaps to be transformed by the encounter. Abraham Coles's "Sabbath at Niagara" certainly expresses this belief. Other devout travelers recorded their aspirations and experiences in the *Album of the Table Rock,* a kind of open register kept near the brink of the falls in the 1830s and 1840s. Because anyone could write in the *Album,* it provides valuable evidence of the sentiments and thoughts of Niagara's less prominent visitors. Unfortunately, we often know nothing about these individuals beyond what they reveal through their words. George Menzies, for instance, wrote that he had been lured all the way from Scotland hoping to "gaze on glories that might wake to prayer / All but the hopeless victim of despair."[50] And Rev. John Dowling of Providence, a religious writer of some success, described the spiritual transformation he prayed would overtake him while contemplating Niagara's rainbow:

> And as I gaze, in yon bless'd world, for ever,
> Thus sweetly may the fountains of my soul,
> Be broken up; and tears, luxurious tears,
> Of joy and gratitude for ever flow.[51]

To people like Rev. Dowling, Niagara was too fantastic to have happened by chance. Surely, they believed, the creator had put it here for a purpose. Some saw that purpose as didactic—it might simply be meant to show the puniness of human beings—while others thought it had a symbolic lesson to teach. One visitor from the 1830s, who simply signed the initials A.R.P., found in the falls a symbol for the purity of faith:

So costly churches and the glittering dome,
May prove that wealth hath found religion's home,
But Nature's wonders must inspire the heart,
That worships God by love and not by art.

Vain are the hymns that feeble choirs may raise,
Compared with Nature's all pervading praise;
So like the praise of Niagara's roar,
Our praise should rise from this for evermore.[52]

The religious view of Niagara received official recognition when Pope Pius IX, at the urging of Archbishop Lynch of Toronto, established a "pilgrim shrine" at Niagara Falls in 1861. This action bestowed upon Niagara—in the eyes of the Catholic Church at least—the same status as the most famous of Old World pilgrim centers. In a pastoral letter written several years later, Archbishop Lynch described his aspirations for the new pilgrim center: "In Europe there are many sanctuaries, but few in this new world. Niagara will be one, and first of the most famous where God will be adored on the spot in which He manifests Himself in such incomparable majesty and grandeur."[53] Lynch issued the pastoral letter on the occasion of his founding of a Carmelite monastery at Niagara Falls: "A place more fitting for such an institution could hardly be found," he wrote; "God Himself has made the selection."[54]

Many of those who traveled to Niagara in the nineteenth century called themselves pilgrims out of a reverence for nature rather than out of a religious conviction. An anonymous visitor writing in the *Album of the Table Rock*, for example, described Niagara as "Nature's loudest voice speaking to the soul through the medium of those ever rushing waters—the holy place of the earth!"[55] Such travelers believed that they could personally experience the sacredness of nature at Niagara. The British novelist and humorist Anthony Trollope offered a prescription to those seeking such an experience in his book, *North America* (1863). With uncharacteristic passion, he wrote:

To realize Niagara, you must sit there till you see nothing else than that which you have come to see. You will hear nothing else, and think of nothing else. At length you will be at one with the tumbling river before you. You will find yourself among the waters as though you belonged to them. The cool, liquid green will run through your veins, and the voice of the cataract will be the expression of your own heart. You will fall as the bright waters fall, rushing down into your new world with no hesitation and with no dismay; and you will rise again as the spray rises, bright, beautiful, and pure. Then you will flow away in your course to the uncompassed, distant, and eternal ocean.[56]

Travelers who believed nature was sacred saw Niagara as a kind of sanctuary, like the religious pilgrim center, outside the confines of normal life. "Living at Niagara was not like ordinary life," reported the English traveler George Carlisle in an 1850 lecture; "the whole of existence there has a dreamy but not a frivolous impress; you feel that you are not in the common world, but in its sublimest temple."[57] As the nineteenth century progressed, those who shared Carlisle's view of Niagara became more and more distressed at what was happening to the place. Mills crowded the American shore, extending even onto the islands of the upper rapids. High fees were charged at all points where one might view the spectacle. Hackmen and hustlers of every sort became infamous for pestering visitors. To those who considered Niagara a sanctuary of nature, these human intrusions were a virtual desecration.

Eventually, a broadbased movement to preserve the falls began to gather force. After an extended struggle, the State of New York established a small reservation in 1885, and the Province of Ontario followed suit in 1887.[58] James C. Carter, a prominent attorney who dedicated the American reservation, said he had come, representing the state of New York, "to declare that the awful symbol of Infinite Power, in whose dread presence we stand—these visions of Infinite Beauty here unfolded to the eye, are not a property but a shrine," and to confess "the duty of guardianship imposed by her over the place; that she marked out the boundaries of the sanctuary, expels from the interior all ordinary human pursuits and claims, so that visitors and pilgrims from near or far may come hither, and be permitted to behold, to love, to worship, to adore."[59]

Carter's statement captures the pilgrim's image perfectly. The pilgrim center was outside of the ordinary realm. To be idealized, it had to be placed in a no-man's land, separate from "ordinary human pursuits." The characteristics of the common world did not apply to this no-man's land; here one might encounter "Infinite Power" and "Infinite Beauty." Niagara's image coincided with that of the pilgrim center and was equally embraced by those who saw the falls as an expression of God and those who saw it as an expression of nature.

It would be misleading, however, to imply that there were no differences between the traveler's image of Niagara and the pilgrim's image of the pilgrim center. For one thing, the very idea that purely natural phenomenon could be holy would have been entirely foreign to a medieval traveler. Donald Howard has pointed out another difference. Traditional pilgrims thought of their journey as a one-way trip that ultimately led, like life itself, to another world. But most nineteenth-century travelers who called themselves pilgrims wanted only a brief immersion in this other world; they were intent upon returning to everyday life with, if nothing else, their memories.[60]

The traveler's view that Niagara was extraordinary began as an idealization from afar; it began in imagination. But when government and church authorities sanctioned this view, it found a more concrete embodiment in the visible landscape itself: parks were established; a monastery was built. Unlikely as it seems, the carnival atmosphere at Niagara may be another way that this view found embodiment in the landscape. Although indubitably profane, the carnival atmosphere made Niagara tangibly different from ordinary places.

Throughout the nineteenth century, Niagara's visitors were greeted with exotic markets, horror museums, and an endless series of stunts. Daring men and women walked and rode bicycles on tightropes stretched over the river. Others challenged the rapids or the cataract itself in barrels and giant rubber balls. In 1872 a local promoter staged a reenactment of an Indian burial and buffalo hunt. He hired Wild Bill Hickock and Buffalo Bill Cody to transport Indians and live buffaloes from the Midwest and to act in the extravaganza.[61] P. T. Barnum also recognized the possibilities of the place and tried to purchase Goat Island—which straddles the escarpment between the American and Horseshoe Falls—as a permanent site for his big top.[62] Although Barnum was unsuccessful in his enterprise, others succeeded in institutionalizing the circus at Niagara.

The contemporary visitor will find several centers offering exotic shopping and entertainment. There is Circus World, where one can see "the Fat Lady, the Fire Eater, the Snake Charmer," and a "Giant Gorilla." There is Pyramid Place, with "Canada's largest movie screen," exotic shops, animals, and circus acts. There is Marineland, with its killer whales, dolphins, seals, elephants, tigers, and "a forest full of bears, a 'Zillion' pettable deer, a Buffalo herd, a pride of Lions; all less than a mile from the Falls." There is Maple Leaf Village, where one can ride the "largest wheel in the Western Hemisphere." There is the Skylon Tower with its indoor amusement park and its numerous shops featuring handicrafts and "irresistible" gifts "from around the world." And if you have just arrived from overseas, there is no need to go to a bank; the Skylon will exchange your money on the spot if you are from Britain, France, West Germany, Australia, or Japan.[63]

This same sort of side show surrounds most modern tourist attractions, and in some cases such as Disneyworld, the carnival has become the attraction itself. The landscape of Niagara Falls was simply the nineteenth century's most extreme example of a paradox. "Nowhere else in the United States," John Sears observes, "could you find the popular and the democratically genteel, Coney Island and Central Park, P. T. Barnum and Frederick Law Olmsted in such vivid juxtaposition."[64]

On the face of it, all of this seems incongruous with the pilgrim's reverence. Yet Victor Turner points out that fairs and exotic markets always crowded around the great pilgrim churches of Europe. It was as if these activities, like pilgrimage itself, were outside the realm of ordinary life. They all belonged together, as Turner notes, "in a place set apart."[65] The core of both the traveler's view of Niagara and the pilgrim's view of the pilgrim center is just this image of a place set apart from the rest of the world.

In the second half of the nineteenth century, Niagara Falls became a favored destination for a new kind of travel, the honeymoon—or, as it was more commonly called then, the wedding journey. The honeymoon was, and to some extent still is, an important rite of passage. Victor Turner argues that there is also "a *rite de passage,* even an initiatory ritual character about pilgrimage."[66] Initiates in a rite of passage are temporarily removed from the structures of social life, and in this structureless state, this social limbo, they undergo a ritual transformation. Traditional pilgrims also temporarily withdrew from the usual structures of society: ideally, at least, all pilgrims were equal. And they, too, often hoped to be transformed before they returned.

Marriage, particularly in the nineteenth century, was certainly a momentous transition. In a recent study of courtship and marriage in nineteenth-century America, Ellen Kate Rothman has found that most individuals anticipated marriage as a decisive break from their former lives. As an illustration, she quotes from the diary of Florence Finch, who remembered looking into the mirror on the morning of her wedding day: ". . . with a nostalgic surge of feeling that almost overwhelmed my will I waved my hand at the reflection and said 'Goodbye.' It was truly a foreknowledge, for never again was I quite the same person I had been before, never again did life present to me the same face to which I had been accustomed."[67]

The honeymoon was thus a hiatus between two life situations—a temporal no-man's land. Honeymooners had left behind a structured world, and when they returned to it, their place in that world would be radically different. Niagara, a place set apart from this ordinary, structured world, was an appropriate venue for this transformation. Consider William Dean Howells's comments on Niagara in his 1888 novel, *Their Wedding Journey:* "I think with tenderness of all the lives that have opened so fairly there. . . . Elsewhere there are carking cares of business and of fashion, there are age, and sorrow, and heartbreak; but here only youth, faith, rapture."[68] The same image that attracted nineteenth-century travelers, made Niagara an appropriate site for a wedding journey.

The Distant Niagara

In an age dominated by railroad travel, Niagara Falls became "the honeymoon capital of the world," a designation local promoters still employ. Although no other single place has been more closely associated with the honeymoon, the rise of automobile and air travel have left Niagara as only one among many destinations that offer bridal suites with heart-shaped tubs. Yet it was Niagara Falls that set the tone: the honeymoon was to be an escape to a place palpably distinct from one's ordinary surroundings. To Americans, this has often meant a natural place such as the Poconos or a Caribbean island. The honeymoon is still a rite of passage, but the life transition it marks has become less abrupt. Moreover, the moment of consummation is now rarely delayed until the honeymoon. A remarkable number of American couples, nevertheless, still feel the need to outwardly symbolize their new lives together with a ceremonial journey that removes them from their everyday worlds.

Beyond the edge of the known world, medieval Europeans had imagined a world unlike their own, a world that corresponded to their deepest earthly fears and their loftiest earthly hopes. To venture beyond that threshold was to leave behind order and limitations. Out there one might find a fountain of youth or riches or even the earthly paradise itself, but one might also encounter enormous whirlpools or the satanic hordes of Gog and Magog. When early modern Europeans looked beyond this threshold, their hopes outweighed their fears. The world beyond stirred their imaginations. From out of that world came the first descriptions of Niagara Falls in the seventeenth century. Like the *terra incognita* in which it had been discovered, Niagara was something to stimulate the imagination. Europeans imagined it from the beginning as a fabulous waterfall.

When canals and railroads made Niagara accessible to millions, many began to regard such a trip as a pilgrimage. They viewed Niagara as a traditional pilgrim center, a sacred place where one might transcend the limits of the mundane world. This too was a view from a distance nurtured in imagination. For some travelers, the sight of Niagara Falls did not match their expectations. Nevertheless, understanding the Niagara that people imagined from afar is essential to understanding the Niagara that they have actually created.

This chapter has focused on the way people imagined Niagara across the threshold of space. But for some visitors, Niagara was itself a threshold. They believed you could stand on one side of this threshold and look beyond the brink to the other. For these people, as I demonstrate in the next chapter, Niagara Falls was a stimulus to imagination even without the veil of distance.

three

DEATH AT NIAGARA

Many visitors have studied the landscape of Niagara Falls as a kind of text to be interpreted, as did the American writer Margaret Fuller, who came to Niagara in 1843 "to woo the mighty meaning from the scene."[1] Visitors, particularly in the nineteenth century, read a bewildering array of meanings in Niagara's landscape. In this chapter I examine a subset of these readings of Niagara Falls—those that find in Niagara's landscape a metaphor for death. I draw the evidence primarily from poems, novels, travel journals, and other texts written by Niagara's visitors. However, the metaphor of death is also manifest in the landscape that humans have created around the waterfall. At Niagara Falls there are tangible institutions and behavioral traditions related directly and indirectly to the symbolism of death. These features of the cultural landscape are another kind of text that can be understood in conjunction with the written texts.

This chapter begins by tracing the manner in which death came to be symbolically associated with Niagara Falls, partly through the presence of actual danger and death. Archival evidence and written accounts demonstrate that many visitors regarded Niagara not only as a symbol of death but also as a stage on which to act out individual responses to death. These responses can only be understood within a broader historical and cultural matrix, which the second part of this chapter explores. A fervid public discourse on the meaning of death raged throughout the Victorian period. Although its terms of reference were certainly traditional, the evidence at Niagara shows that this discourse allowed for a remarkable degree of latitude in imaginative speculation. Nevertheless, both the visions of death and the way people shaped Niagara's landscape in accordance with those visions must be interpreted in terms of prevailing cultural beliefs about death. The final section examines the death metaphor in detail. Certain physical features of Niagara Falls—the brink, the plunge, the abyss, the rising mist, and the rainbow—have been consistently regarded in terms of prevailing notions of the afterlife. By understanding the individual elements of the metaphor, we can interpret certain alterations of the human landscape at Niagara Falls.

Niagara Falls is a place of death. As literal proof, there is a family of daredevils at Niagara Falls who claim that they have pulled more than 500 corpses from the lower river since the turn of the century.[2] This "River of Death,"[3] as some have called the Niagara, began claiming victims at least as long ago as the eighteenth century, when—we learn from the diary of Mrs. Simcoe, wife of Upper Canada's first lieutenant-governor—eight British soldiers were accidentally swept to their deaths.[4] As many as fifty-three victims in a single year have been "rolled and hurled," as the American writer William Dean Howells put it, "headlong on to the cataract's brink, and out of the world."[5] Here was a place that made people aware of their mortality and aroused their curiosity about the afterlife.

As early as the 1830s, death had become part of the lure of Niagara. Guidebooks repeated the gruesome details of accidents, suicides, murders, and narrow escapes.[6] A favorite tale was that of a young man who, while playing with a child near the brink of the falls, pretended to throw her in. She accidentally slipped through his arms, and when he tried to save her, both were "hurried into eternity" as one visitor described it.[7] In the two earliest novels that feature Niagara, the hero dies at the falls. The first of these, *Atala* (1801)—written by the famous French romanticist Chateaubriand—reaches its climax when the young Indian heroine takes poison and dies in her lover's arms. In a concluding scene that takes place years later, the narrator meets an Indian woman who has come to Niagara to bury her infant son. With her comes her exiled tribe carrying the bones of their ancestors, among which are the bones of the heroine who had died at Niagara many years before.[8] Similarly, James Fenimore Cooper, who helped establish the American tradition of writing about nature and the wilderness, used Niagara Falls as the setting of a final battle in *The Spy* (1821); the patriotic hero not only dies but is also buried at Niagara.[9] Later, the theme of death entered the popular fiction of Niagara Falls. A series of five-cent detective mysteries, published near the turn of the century, used the falls as a backdrop for murder[10]—a device repeated more recently in Henry Hathaway's film, *Niagara,* which starred Marilyn Monroe.[11]

Partly because of the stories of death that made their way into popular lore, many have found it difficult, while standing at the brink of the falls, to ignore the spectre of death. Charles Dudley Warner, the urbane Hartford editor, essayist, and travel writer, described the brink this way in an 1887 novel—one of his few attempts at fiction:

> And there every islet, every rock, every point has its legend of terror; here a boat lodged with a man in it, and after a day and a night of vain attempts to rescue him, thousands of people saw him take the frightful leap, throwing up his hands as he went over; here a young woman slipped, and was instantly whirled away out of life; and from that point more than one dazed or frantic visitor had taken the suicidal leap. Death was so near here and so easy.[12]

As the British romanticist Mrs. Jameson commented in 1836, people felt the nearness of death because of "the immediate danger, the consciousness that anything caught within its verge is inevitably hurried to a swift destination, swallowed up, annihilated."[13]

Given the presence of real danger and the accumulation of stories and legends of death, it is not surprising that the falls were eventually treated as a metaphor for death itself. James K. Liston, a poet from western Upper Canada, presents the basis of the metaphor in his "Niagara Falls: A Poem in Three Cantos" (1843):

> The slope of life, where none can retrograde
> A single step, but must each moment live;
> Live but to move right onward to the brink
> Of Death's huge precipice invisible,
> Unfenced, uncharted in the maps of life
> Because of its most strange ubiquity.[14]

W. A. Boord, a late nineteenth-century Australian visitor, calls Niagara "the very emblem . . . of unchanging, inevitable death."[15] "Down this predestined course," he writes, "ton follows ton as remorselessly as human generations speed to the great Unknown."[16] The metaphor even appears in an 1888 insurance advertisement:

> The water does not flow over "Niagara Falls" more steadily nor more resistlessly than the stream of living humanity passes over from this world to the abode of the silent majority; therefore be worldly wise and provide a future support for those who depend on your now strong arm. Insure your life in Massachusetts Mutual Life Insurance Co.[17]

Niagara Falls became a grim reminder of the ultimate limitedness of the human condition. "Here is the spot of all others upon the broad earth," wrote Thomas Rolph, a British physician and bureaucrat who served in Upper Canada between 1832 and 1839, "where the nothingness of human pride comes home upon the heart; where . . . its hard wrestlings with the doom to which it is fated, sink into their native insignificance."[18]

But the human heart does not always respond the same way to "the doom to which it is fated." Thus, Niagara is a stage upon which many responses to death have been played out. Some fought against death at Niagara. Using all of their strength and ingenuity, they pulled themselves or others back from the brink. One of these was Edward Di Ruscio, a twenty-year-old Chicagoan who, in 1951, swam fifty feet into the river to rescue a woman just a hundred feet above the American Falls.[19] Literally hundreds of people, most of them attempting suicide, have been rescued at the brink.[20] Others defied death at Niagara. They walked or rode bicycles on tightropes stretched over the river; they breached its waters in barrels and giant rubber balls.[21] In 1974, Philippe Petit, the fleetingly famous French aerialist, planned to traverse the falls on a wire. When asked about the dangerous stunt, he replied: "In the world of the possible, it is just before the impossible."[22]

Those who attempted feats close to the impossible often lost their taste for defiance. Annie Edson Taylor, the first person to survive a trip over the falls in a barrel, warned after her 1901 ordeal: "If it was with my dying breath I would caution anyone against attempting the feat. I will never go over the Falls again. I would sooner walk up to the mouth of a cannon, knowing it was going to blow me to pieces, than make another trip over the Falls."[23]

In the mid-nineteenth century, Joel Robinson was known as the most intrepid and resourceful of Niagara rivermen. He had rescued so many from the vicinity of the falls that people called him the "Navigator of the Rapids." When presented with the opportunity to pilot the then-retired steamer *Maid of the Mist* through the lower rapids in 1867, Robinson felt an "irrepressible desire" to take the challenge. When the ship entered the turbulent water, it was battered and slashed with such fury that Robinson feared it would immediately disintegrate. The ship survived but Joel Robinson, according to his wife, "was twenty years older when he came home that day than when he went out."[24] A contemporary local historian further described this transformation:

> He decided to abandon the water and he advised his sons to venture no more about the rapids. Both his manner and his appearance were changed. Calm and deliberate before, he became thoughtful and serious afterward. He had been borne, as it were, in the arms of a power so mighty that its impress was stamped on his features and on his mind. Through a slightly opened door he had seen a vision which awed and subdued him.[25]

There were many others who, in their defiance of death, knocked too loudly on that door that Robinson had peeked through. One of these was an English barber named George Henry Stephens. In 1919, his oak barrel "smashed like an egg" beneath the Horseshoe Falls; only his tattooed arm was recovered. Another was the Greek chef George Stathakis: his wood and steel barrel became his coffin after a twenty-two-hour pummelling beneath the falls in 1930.[26] Finally, in 1957, a man claiming to be God arrived at Niagara Falls; as several of his followers looked on, he attempted to "walk on the water" above the American Falls. Needless to say, he found the footing hazardous and was swept over the brink in seconds.[27]

Many have come to Niagara not to defy death but to seek it out. For those who have felt beaten down by this world, Niagara has provided a rapid and certain exit. A recent study concludes that Niagara Falls has seen far more suicides than any other place in North America, including the Golden Gate Bridge; "year after year, (at least) one person a month uses the falls to kill himself."[28]

Yet, many who ended their lives at Niagara had not arrived with that intention. Seized by a sudden impulse at the brink, they left this world without apparent revulsion or remorse. In a recent documentary film, a woman who works at a concession stand near the brink spoke of the numerous suicides she had witnessed: "The strangest thing about people who jump over the falls is that they don't even think. Like I said, the one woman was waving at everybody as she floated on her back over the falls."[29] A Toronto woman recently pulled from the river explained that she had been captivated by the "overpowering roar that became louder and louder in my ears."[30] The chief of Canada's Niagara Parks Police says that many who are rescued "tell us that they had no intention of committing suicide, but they still had this feeling of the attraction of the water."[31] Until recently, local authorities have hesitated to acknowledge the suicide problem, fearing that publicity would damage the tourism industry. Now, special blue phones have been placed at the most popular suicide sites along the American side of the river (figure 2). These phones offer a direct connection to a suicide prevention counseling center. In

2. Suicide prevention measures at Prospect Point, Niagara Falls,
New York. (Photo by author)

addition, an eight-foot-tall suicide fence stands at the observation
tower at Prospect Point.

These suicides were not the only ones who felt "the attraction
of the water." Many nonsuicidal travelers have also described an
attraction, even an urge to jump in.[32] T. R. Preston, a Toronto-
nian who visited the falls in 1842, nearly succumbed to "an
attracting influence," which he compared to "the fascination
exercised by the lodestone or the eye of a rattlesnake."[33] George
William Curtis, a prominent orator, editor, and close friend of
Emerson, tried to analyze this hypnotic phenomenon: "It flows
so tranquilly, is so unimpatient of the mighty plunge, that it woos
and woos you to lay down your head upon its breast and slide into
dreamless sleep."[34] In 1834, Harriet Beecher Stowe visited Niagara Falls and recorded this often-expressed sentiment:

> I felt as if I could have *gone over* with the waters; it would be so
> beautiful a death; there could be no fear in it. I felt the rock
> tremble under me with a sort of joy. I was so maddened that I
> could have gone too, if it had gone.[35]

One way of interpreting this acquiescence is to postulate, with Freud, a death instinct. The "sort of joy" Stowe felt could then be related to the death principle: an instinctual desire "to return to the peace of the inorganic world."[36] It is also possible to see in this attraction the same dissatisfaction with human limitations that leads the daredevil to acts of defiance. Instead of capitulation to a state of peace, we might interpret it as an urge to extend the human world beyond death. While the daredevil challenges the limit, others see the limit as a threshold or a gateway to an unlimited world. Each tests limitedness in a different way.

We can observe the similarities between defiance and fascination at Niagara most clearly in the character of Francis Abbott, a man who was apparently given to both. Abbott arrived at the village of Niagara Falls, New York, in June 1829.[37] Although he intended to stay only a few days, "a mystic chain," as one poet put it, "round his soul was wove."[38] He never left the falls again. Settling in a rude cabin near the brink, Abbott became known as the "Hermit of the Falls." "In the wildest hours of the night," we learn from the journal of one contemporary, "he was often found walking alone and undismayed, in the most dangerous places near the falls."[39] At that time a large beam extended out about ten feet over the Horseshoe Falls from the American side. Francis would often walk this beam for hours at a time, or hang from its end by hands or feet, or descend from a rope "like a spider from its thread, over the awful gulf beneath him."[40] Although some considered this act a "morbid enthusiasm,"[41] it has fascinated many who have since written about Niagara.[42]

Many of these writers sentimentalized the story of the Hermit.[43] Yet he remained a compelling figure because of his apparent attitude toward death: he seemed more curious than afraid. James Bird, an English visitor, in 1837 wrote of the Hermit's beam-walking: "Poised on his foot above the gulf beneath / One slippery step between himself and death."[44] A later historian described the feat this way: "On this [beam] he would walk with folded arms, apparently oblivious of the danger and thoughts of the awful death that seemed to be reaching up for him out of the mighty depths below."[45] By coming nearer and nearer to death, he was proving that one could bring the human world closer to death than most people cared to try. Perhaps he imagined something beyond death that was more compelling than life on this side.

The Hermit had a habit of bathing in the river, summer and winter. One day in 1831, he failed to return to the shore. It is still unclear whether Francis Abbott's death was a suicide, but if it was, we might surmise that it signified less a rejection of this world than an attraction to something imagined beyond it. This remains speculation, however, since Abbott destroyed everything he wrote.

The fascination with death exhibited by people like Francis Abbott and Harriet Beecher Stowe would have been unthinkable in an earlier age. Niagara was, in many ways, a lightning rod for nineteenth-century enthusiasms, and death became one of that century's most spirited obsessions.

Death is obviously something that binds people of all eras. As Arthur Koestler has put it, we are all "faced with the untractable paradox of consciousness emerging from nothingness and returning to nothingness."[46] But the way people in the Western world have viewed death has changed dramatically through time. In the twentieth century, there is a horror associated with death and consequently a desire to separate the dead from the living. Cemeteries, for example, are clearly marked off from the sphere of normal life. In contrast, Philippe Aries has found that the medieval cemetery was a distinctly public place—a site of dancing, gambling, juggling, sport, and business. Death itself was marked by a simple public ceremony. In Aries's words, "death was both familiar and near, evoking no great fear or awe."[47]

Beginning in the twelfth and thirteenth centuries, a new emphasis on individuality altered both the perception and the observance of death. This change began with the idea of a personal judgment at the moment of death. By the fifteenth century, the personal judgment had become a trial, a final temptation. In the last moment, it was believed, one's life flashed before one's eyes, and one's "attitude at that moment would give his biography its final meaning, its conclusion."[48] Several other developments in the Western way of dying parallel this emphasis on the individual's last moment.

From the fifth century until the thirteenth, burial had been anonymous, but burial customs gradually became more individualized. Inscriptions reappeared first on the tombs of saints and royalty. By the eighteenth century, they had spread to the middle class. In the art and literature of the fourteenth through the sixteenth centuries, the horrifying figure of the partly decomposed cadaver began to appear. In Aries's view, emphasis on the individual life had transformed death from something natural to something strikingly horrible.[49]

This idea that death was not a natural part of life—that it represented a rupture, a break from the familiar world—helps to explain a further development: the association of death and eroticism, which emerged in the art and literature of the sixteenth century. Aries writes:

> Like the sexual act, death was henceforth increasingly thought of as a transgression which tears man from his daily life, from rational society, from his monotonous work, in order to make him undergo a paroxism, plunging him into an irrational, violent, and beautiful world.

The erotico-macabre themes in this art and literature prepared the way for what Aries calls the "romantic death," to be found, for instance, in the writings of Twain and the Brontës. "The very idea of death moved them," but their "morbid fascination," Aries suggests, "may merely be a sublimation . . . of the erotico-macabre phantasms of the preceding period."[50]

This growing awareness of, and fascination with, individual death culminated in the nineteenth century, and was exhibited in a number of ways. First, there was the rise of spiritualism in the 1840s, beginning in the United States but soon spreading to Europe.[51] Second, there was the fervid public debate, which raged between 1830 and 1880, concerning the meaning and the very existence of hell. Third, there were numerous books on the subject of death which enjoyed great popularity; they bore titles such as *The Grave, Meditations against the Tombs, Death-Bed Scenes,* and *The Future State.* This obsession even affected Britain's royal family; Prince Albert and the Queen read together a volume called *Heaven Our Home,* which described heaven as an "etherialised, luminous, material habitation." Fourth, there were the immensely popular "Judgment Pictures" of John Martin. The first two canvases depicted scenes of apocalyptic terror, and the third portrayed a "celestial landscape in iridescent blues and golds peopled with white robed figures."[52] These paintings were first exhibited in London in 1855 as "the most sublime and extraordinary pictures in the world." Later they drew large crowds throughout Britain and North America.

A good deal of nineteenth-century literature seems to be informed by this fascination with death and what lies beyond death. This is particularly true of the Gothic tradition and what has been labeled "Dark Romanticism" or "Negative Romanticism."[53] The romantics made no attempt to hide their fascination with death, nor even their fascination with hell itself. They read Milton's and especially Dante's depiction of the next world from a new perspective. Clearly Dante, Milton, and their respective readers had been fascinated with the diabolical as well as the angelic, but they had always evaluated the former in the traditional negative terms. The romantics had no such traditional obligations; Lucifer's defiance, moreover, appealed to their Promethean urges. "The Dark Romantic hero," writes G. R. Thompson, "by working in and through evil and darkness, by withholding final investment of belief in either good or evil, ... perhaps attains some Sisyphean or Promethean semblance of victory."[54]

Edgar Allan Poe was perhaps more obsessed with death that any other nineteenth-century writer. Harry Levin describes this preoccupation as "his morbid curiosity, his restless desire to penetrate the ultimate secret." What Poe really desired has been suggestively characterized by George Poulet as a state of "posthumous consciousness."[55] Poe's immense international popularity suggests that, to many people, this desire did not seem alien. Freud once commented: "Whenever we make the attempt to imagine our own death . . . we really survive as spectators."[56] Similarly, Rowell notes that among those most vehemently committed to the existence of hellfire, not one "seriously considered it, in all its horror, as a possibility for himself."[57] Death can be fascinating if one is still here looking over at it. A certain separation is necessary; it must be remote. Many of those who travelled to Niagara, particularly in the nineteenth century, seemed to share Poe's fascination with death.

Geoffrey Rowell claims that the growing stature of science eventually caused many to abandon belief in a sequel to death. With characteristic turn-of-the-century optimism, William Gladstone commented that the doctrine of hell had been "relegated . . . to the far-off corners of the Christian mind . . . there to sleep in deep shadow as a thing needless in our enlightened and progressive age."[58] However, according to some twentieth-century interpreters, the intense nineteenth-century awareness of death has not been overcome but merely repressed.[59] Given the breadth and intensity of this discourse on death, it is not surprising that the issue should appear at the site of another nineteenth-century obsession—Niagara Falls, where nearly the full range of discourse finds expression.

The death metaphor appears at Niagara Falls partly, of course, because of the presence of actual danger and the record of suicides and accidental deaths. But the elaboration of the metaphor derives its impetus from the vigorous discourse on death bubbling in Niagara's wider cultural context.

Those who have read a metaphor of death in Niagara's natural landscape have used their experience at the falls to explore the nature of death. Gazing from the brink of Niagara Falls has moved them to imagine what the experience of dying would be like. A good part of the descriptive literature they have produced could be characterized as imaginative speculation on the afterworld. Although these visitors try to read the landscape like a text with a definite meaning, the richness of the metaphor has allowed this text to serve as a locus for imagination, a catalyst for exploring the nature of death. What these visitors have brought to the landscape, rather than something inherent in it, is obviously key to their readings. They have brought, first of all, knowledge of stories and legends of death and perhaps some familiarity with the writings of others who have seen the metaphor of death in Niagara's landscape. Their readings, therefore, are complexly intertextual. Many of their speculations on the afterlife take their structure from the prevalent literary and theological sources of Victorian Christian culture, but often, as we shall see, they imaginatively develop that structure in highly unorthodox ways.

This exploration of the metaphor of death will proceed sequentially through the elements of the river landscape. There is a fair amount of agreement among a host of writers on the symbolic meaning that should be attributed to the brink, the plunge, the abyss, the rising mist, and the rainbow—all in relation to the theme of death. What follows, therefore, is a sort of geography of Niagara's metaphor of death.

If life is construed as a river that will ultimately plunge over a precipice, the brink of that precipice is the boundary line between life and death, a place where one could perhaps look beyond, if only in imagination. William Chambers Wilbor, a scholarly Methodist clergyman who served in several western New York cities, wrote in 1896:

> There in the solitude and on the brink
> Of thy unseen abyss, with darkness filled,
> The sound of many waters and the ghostly
> Sheet of foam above thee, are speech and forms
> Of other worlds to me. Amazed, and with
> 'Bated breath, I seem to stand, upon the
> Verge of time, alone with thy creator.[60]

James K. Liston's "Niagara Falls: A Poem in Three Cantos" (1843) is especially rich in these images of Niagara. Again, it is the brink itself which the early Canadian writer variously names "Death's huge precipice," "Death's dark door-posts," the "frontiers of Life's bounded territories," and "that mysterious line / That separates eternity from time." Liston argues that people ought to be more curious about

>   . . . what is going on
> On further side of that most narrow line
> Between the visible and the unseen worlds!

For Liston, apparently, a trip to Niagara would necessarily inspire this curiosity. It would set one to wondering whether to expect "the palm of victory, or the blasts of flame."[61] Many writers, especially those with a religious purpose in mind, emphasized the soul-searching that the brink inspired. Archbishop Lynch of Toronto, for instance, wrote in 1876 that Niagara's brink should recall to the individual "his own last leap" when "the soul shall tremble on the precipice of eternity," and he reminded his reader that "death holds many a deep secret of a good or ill-spent life."[62] The symbolism of the brink as the final moment of life connects the metaphor with the numerous examples of real deaths at Niagara. The eight-foot fence on the observation tower and the emergency phones are further manifestations of this connection.

If the brink of Niagara is the final moment of life, then the plunge is a fall from life, a fall into death. Some visitors have called it an endless fall, a fall into eternity. An anonymous poem published in 1879 focuses on the plunge:

> I saw, I heard. The liquid thunder
> Went pouring to its foaming hell
> And it fell,
> Ever, ever fell
> Into the invisible abyss that opened under.[63]

Death is a moment of transformation. The plunging waters make an appropriate metaphor of transformation as, for example, in this description written by Henry James after an 1871 visit:

> Even the roll of the white batteries at the base seems fixed and poised and ordered, and in the vague middle zone of difference between the flood as it falls and the mist as it rises you imagine a mystical meaning—the passage of body to soul, of matter to spirit, of human to divine.[64]

An unusual story should be mentioned here because, in terms of the dominant symbology of death at Niagara, it intervenes in the plunge just above the abyss. Linda de Kowalewska Fulton, the author of the story, was a prominent Buffalo woman known for her lectures on local history. Her book, *Nadia: The Maid of the Mist* (1901), is a tale of death, but there is little horror to it. At the moment of death, victims are snatched away to a special Niagara limbo. Fulton's main character is a young man who comes to Niagara thinking of suicide. While there, he has a dream that a beautiful maiden is calling for help in the river. When he attempts to save her, she reveals that she has been acting and leads him behind the falls to a spacious chamber ruled by Aeolus, god of winds. There he discovers Indians, voyageurs, soldiers, youths, and maidens—"the spirits of all who have gone over the great falls, or who have been drowned in the river or the rapids below, and thus become vassals of the water king until the Judgement Day." The young man questions several Niagara victims about the circumstances of their deaths and their state of satisfaction under the water king. One of the voyageurs responds that he "cannot complain," and adds: "This is much better than the purgatory I had looked forward to as my just deserts."[65] The victims of the river have somehow managed to escape the abyss that was seen as inescapable by nearly all who commented on death at Niagara. Within the context of this literature, therefore, the story seems anticlimatic. In terms of the wider metaphor, it is significant that Fulton locates her limbo behind the falling water. The plunge is still a moment of transformation, a falling out of this world, but both the fall and the transformation are arrested short of entry into another world. This tale also indicates that individuals could sometimes imaginatively transcend predominant images of the afterlife and create unorthodox alternatives.

Entering the abyss, we break into a new dimension. George William Curtis, in a typically compelling passage, described it this way:

> Looking over into the abyss, we behold nothing below, we hear only a slow, constant thunder; and, bewildered in the mist, dream that the Cataract has cloven the earth to its centre, and that, pouring its waters into the fervent inner heat, they hiss into spray, and overhang the fated Fall, the sweat of its agony.[66]

Symbolically, the abyss is out of this world and the limits of this world no longer apply. We can see this in two ways. First, the abyss is unmeasurable: John C. Lord, a Presbyterian minister from Buffalo, described it in 1869 as "fathomless as Hell";[67] James K. Liston called it a "boundless, bottomless eternity."[68] Second, we find that things can change into their opposites. In the description of Nicholas Woods, the official writer who accompanied the prince of Wales to North America in 1859, a "hell of waters"[69] becomes a hell of fire. Henry Tudor—another English traveler—also saw both fire and water in the abyss; he described it as "an unearthly cauldron heated by a hidden volcano."[70]

If when we enter the abyss we have left this world, the question remains: What kind of place have we entered? Clearly it is not a good place, even to those who assign it the ultimately beneficial role of purgation. People *experience* it as horrible: what they imagine may derive much of its content from religious and scientific ideas they have learned, but the horror they feel is real and personal. Although many visitors have remarked that Niagara's abyss is something only a Dante or a Milton could describe,[71] these visitors clearly could imagine that abyss themselves. Consider this experience recorded in the journal of Henry Tudor who visited Niagara Falls in 1834:

> . . . when I turned my eyes to the curling masses of ever-rising vapour issuing from the turbulently-boiling surface, that seemed pendent over a hidden volcano, that awful passage from revelations was immediately and most forcibly brought to mind: "And the smoke of their torment ascendeth up for ever and ever, and they have no rest day or night."
>
> I was literally overwhelmed by the unequalled grandeur of this stupendous landscape, by the solemn and absorbing train of thoughts which it had called forth, and by the pitch of overexcitement to which my imagination was wrought; and I felt a chill of secret horror creep through my veins, and curdle, for the moment, my very heart's-blood.[72]

Although Tudor borrows a sentence from Revelations to help him describe the abyss, he clearly has had an experience of feeling a "secret horror" himself.

Visitors have described the abyss at Niagara as "that deep torture-dungeon,"[73] a "valley of darkness,"[74] the "hell of the

Death at Niagara

3. A landscape of death; Castle Dracula, Niagara Falls, Ontario.
(Photo by author)

lost,"[75] and the "bottomless perdition of Milton's fallen angels."[76] The power to imagine terrors seems almost unlimited: the abyss, in Anthony Trollope's view, was "so far down—far as your imagination can sink it."[77] Even for those who saw this abyss as a purgatory which the soul would ultimately leave for a state of eternal bliss, the prospect of death usually remained terrifying. Death, it seems, inevitably involved a taste of hell. Even Jesus, we recall, had his descent into hell.[78]

But people who imagine death with bone-chilling horror may still be attracted to it. Indeed, if it is someone else's death, it may arouse as much curiosity as fear. This fascination with death, even in its most gruesome aspects, is directly illustrated by the numerous horror museums that have clustered at Niagara Falls, successfully playing on the terror that the falls, and in particular the abyss, inspires; for the abyss, understood metaphorically, is the locus of death's deepest horrors. A thorough tourist could begin with a visit to Castle Dracula (figure 3) to see "the recreation of DANTE'S INFERNO, FRANKENSTEIN, a haunting EGYPTIAN MUMMY and many more exceptionally strange characters."[79] At

4. The appeal of Niagara, in part, is related to a fascination
with death. The House of Frankenstein, Niagara Falls, Ontario.
(Photo by author)

the Haunted House the visitor will find, according to promotional literature, "a Ghost in Every Corner, a Skeleton in Every
Closet, Every Kind of Ghoul Imaginable."[80] Next, one might try
the Boris Karloff Wax Museum, the House of Frankenstein
(figure 4), or the Criminal's Hall of Fame. At Ripley's Believe It
or Not! Museum, the tourist may "wonder at the fearsome
ancestor skull, a prize exhibit from New Guinea" and observe the
"world's most unusual graveyard."[81] Then one might "look danger in the eye . . . from a place of safety" at the Niagara
Serpentarium,[82] or visit Louis Tussaud's English Wax Museum
which features "such vivid spectacles as the slow death of Nelson,
whose chest actually heaves as he expires on deck."[83]

These businesses are not a new phenomenon at Niagara. The
Niagara Falls Museum, according to advertisements, claims to be
"the oldest museum in North America."[84] Founded in 1827, this
establishment was worth a visit, in the opinion of one early
traveler, if one wished "to sup full of horrors."[85] The museum's
leading attraction since before the Civil War has been its collec-

tion of Egyptian mummies. As late as 1946, the museum claimed it had the largest such collection in North America.[86] More recently, the operators have added several naturally preserved American Indian "mummies."[87] To link the horror museums to the death metaphor is to recognize that visitors' readings of Niagara's natural landscape are intimately connected with the construction of Niagara's cultural landscape. These museums should also be understood as part of the exotic side-show atmosphere which has long attended Niagara Falls and other prominent travel destinations, be they pilgrim centers or merely vacation magnets. We even find a few horror museums at places as obscure as the Wisconsin Dells. At Niagara the theme of death appears with relatively greater prominence, and this, I suggest, must be understood in terms of the specific metaphor of death articulated by so many visitors.

One of the most terrifying depictions of the afterlife was written by Fitz Hugh Ludlow in his 1857 book *The Hasheesh Eater.* Ludlow was an editor, lawyer, and prolific contributor of short stories, poetry, and criticism to American magazines. His depiction presents a vision of hell—although it is a hell not confined to the abyss. The falls and rapids deeply impressed Ludlow's narrator, and for months after his visit, Niagara haunted the narrator's dreams with visions of a watery death. He found himself "in every variety of posture, helpless, friendless, frequently deserted utterly of every human being, . . . hung suspended over the bellowing chasm." One "most agonizing vision," he wrote, "stamped itself upon my mind with a vividness lingering even while I was awake." In this nightmare he sat at the edge of the cliff next to Niagara Falls, mesmerized by a "singular fascination." A woman sitting beside him repeatedly directed him to gaze into the scene below. Suddenly he felt the rocks slipping beneath him, nearly dragging him down. Realizing that the woman meant to do him harm, he sprang to his feet and grabbed her by the arm:

> I glared into her beautiful icy eyes; I cried out, "Woman! accursed woman! is this your faith?" Now, casting off all disguise, she gave a hollow laugh, and spoke: "Faith! do you look for faith in hell? I would have cast you to the fishes." My

eyes were opened. She said truly. We were indeed in hell, and I had not known it until now. Wearing the same features, with the demoniac instead of the human soul speaking through them—wandering about the same earth, yet aware of no presence but demons like ourselves—lit by the same sky, but hope spoke down from it no more.

I left the she-fiend by the river-bank, and met another as well known to me in the former life. Blandly she wound to my side as if she would entrap me, thinking that I was a new-comer into hell. Knowing her treachery, as if to embrace her I caught her in my arms, and, knitting them about her, strove to crush her out of being. With a look of awful malignity, she loosed one hand, and, tearing open her bosom, disclosed her heart, hissing hot, and pressed it upon my own. "The seal of love I bear thee, my chosen fiend!" she cried. Beneath that flaming signet my heart caught fire; I dashed her away, and then, thank God, awoke.[88]

The narrator's fear of falling into the abyss is shockingly realized when he discovers that Niagara's entire landscape has become "the hell of the lost." This is another example of how the dominant symbology of Niagara's death metaphor could be imaginatively elaborated in quite unorthodox ways.

Some visitors, in spite of their Christian beliefs, have expressed serious doubts about the afterlife their religion promises. A poem written by Thomas Gold Appleton in 1842 provides an example. Appleton, a close friend of Longfellow, perhaps best known as an essayist and travel writer, conveyed his doubts by structuring the poem as two contrasting stanzas. The first stanza gives a daylight view of the falls, full of beauty and "majestic calmness" with "a spirit of mist" returning "to the Heaven it came from." The second stanza begins with an abrupt difference:

As deepens the night, all is changed,
And the joy of my dream is extinguished:
I hear but a measureless prayer,
As of multitudes wailing in anguish;
I see but one fluttering plunge,
As if angels were falling from heaven.

Heaven is now uncapitalized. The stanza concludes:

> As deepens the night, a clear cry
> At times cleaves the boom of the waters;
> Comes with it a terrible sense
> Of suffering extreme and forever.
> The beautiful rainbow is dead,
> And gone are the birds that sang through it,
> The incense so mounting is now
> A stifling, sulphurous vapor,
> The abyss is the hell of the lost
> Hopeless falling to fires everlasting.[89]

Appleton emphasized this dark picture of the abyss by placing it last. "The beautiful rainbow is dead": there is no hope of salvation. But even Appleton—again through the form of his poem—retained an element of ambivalence.

For many interpreters of Niagara's symbolism, the ambivalence has been weighted toward an optimistic view of death. For two late-nineteenth-century poets, even the abyss itself held a positive meaning. Richard Lewis Johnson wrote:

> Nor let thy eyelids ever close,
> In Neptune's arms in sweet repose,
> 'Till all the nations shall disclose,
> > Like thee, Niagara,
>
> A charity as broad and deep
> As is thine own encircling steep,
> Or as thy vortex where we peep
> > Thro' azure mists to heaven.[90]

and Frank B. Palmer:

> Behold, o man, nor shrink aghast in fear!
> > Survey the vortex boiling deep before thee!
> The hand that ope'd the liquid gateway here
> > Hath set the beauteous bow of promise o'er
> > > thee![91]

For these two poets, the abyss held no real terror: it was a vortex that became a tunnel, a passage leading to paradise.

The mist that ascends before the falls has nearly always been interpreted as a sign of hope, an indication that there is more to the afterlife than the abyss. These lines, again by Frank B. Palmer, are typical:

> Though "Hope's bright star" is sometimes pale,
> Let Hope, not fear in man prevail,
> The misty ghost within the veil
> > Proves life's resurrection.[92]

But this resurrection is not a complete one: only a purified soul survives. As James Warner Ward—a scholar, scientist, and director of Buffalo's Grosvenor Library—put it in 1886:

> Frivolous things are cast aside disdainfully;
> Nothing the brink can pass but heaven-lit purity.[93]

And, similarly, Harriet Beecher Stowe wrote: ". . . that beautiful water rising like moonlight, falling as the soul sinks when it dies, to rise refined, spiritualized, and pure."[94]

The English divine and hymnwriter Thomas Grinfield described the mist metaphorically as a "column of ascending incense."[95] These descriptions were often part of a larger metaphor in which the falls was an altar, a temple, or a church. "The cataract of Niagara," wrote Archbishop Lynch of Toronto in 1875, "has been called 'Nature's high altar': the water, as it descends in white foam, the altar-cloth; the spray, the incense; the rainbow the lights of the altar."[96] The rising mist has sometimes inspired a different metaphor when, instead of an altar, the falls is compared to "earth's grandest cathedral," as in these lines by George Houghton:

> Tall above tower and tree looms thy steeple builded of sunshine,
> Mystical steeple, white like a cloud, upyearning toward heaven.[97]

The steeple and the rising incense are both images of yearning for connection with another world. Another symbol of connection—explicitly between heaven and earth—is the rainbow.

That there should be, after the abyss, a rainbow—a bridge to heaven—is of special significance to those purified souls whose "writhing ghosts" are "out from the vortex flung," as Henry T. Blake, a Connecticut lawyer and government official, put it:

> Swift through the glittering archway overspread
> Like radiant portal of immortal hope
> Upsoaring, vanish at the gate of Heaven.[98]

The image of the rainbow as a bridge or portal appears often in the Niagara literature,[99] although the rainbow is not always explicitly a portal to heaven. The Massachusetts traveler Henry Austin, for instance, used the rainbow as a less literal portal in his poem "Niagara" (1900):

> . . . eternal rainbows crown the rocks,
> Halos of Hope, charmed circles of high Faith,
> Commanding entrance through the chasms of Doubt
> To deeps of nobler knowledge and soul-strength.[100]

The rainbow is a traditional sign of hope and of connection between earth and heaven largely because it is also presented as a sign of a covenant. In the Genesis account of the flood, God promises, after the waters have subsided, that "there shall be no flood to destroy the earth again." And, in a passage repeatedly alluded to by Niagara visitors, God gives Noah a sign of this promise:

> Here is the sign of the Covenant I make between myself and you and every living creature with you for all generations: I set my bow in the clouds and it shall be a sign of the Covenant between me and the earth. When I shall gather the clouds over the earth and the bow appears in the clouds, I will recall the Covenant between myself and you and every living creature of every kind. And so the waters shall never again become a flood to destroy all things of flesh. When the bow is in the clouds I shall see it and call to mind the lasting Covenant between God and every living creature of every kind that is found on the earth.[101]

Many writers have interpreted the rainbow at Niagara with explicit reference to this promise. After the deluge descending to the abyss, the rainbow signifies the reestablishment of order, of peace between heaven and earth.

For some visitors, peace has been more than symbolic at Niagara: it has been an experience. Just as the experience of terror at Niagara has its symbolic counterpart in the images of hell and the abyss, so the rainbow as a symbol of peace has its experiential counterpart in the feelings of peace and repose that many visitors have also reported. These feelings of repose have not always been connected with death, redemption, and the symbolism of the rainbow. An English writer, Greville J. Chester, travelling shortly after the Civil War, found peace in the horseshoe itself:

> Standing on the brink of the Canada Fall gazing into the center of the great "horseshoe," where monotony and continuity seem to strive with ever-varying progress, the mind is affected with the deepest sense of peace and repose, and seems to catch the reflected image of Eternity itself. Deep, too, and deeply impressive as are the voices of these many waters, painful and oppressive they nowhere are; and these, too, speak peace to the soul.[102]

One might postulate that even the Horseshoe Falls is connected to the comforting rainbow: it is, after all, an arc-shaped cataract.

The experience of peace has led some visitors directly to thoughts of death and eternal rest. Charles Dickens was one of these. In his 1843 volume, *American Notes for General Circulation,* he wrote:

> It was not until I came on Table Rock, and looked—Great Heaven, on what a fall of bright-green water!—that it came upon me in its full might and majesty.
>
> Then, when I felt how near to my Creator I was standing, the first effect, and the enduring one—instant and lasting—of the tremendous spectacle was Peace. Peace of mind: Tranquility: Calm recollections of the Dead: Great thoughts of Eternal Rest and Happiness: nothing of Gloom and Terror.[103]

The peace that Dickens and other writers experienced at Niagara Falls also found expression in various concrete proposals for the Niagara landscape.

Death at Niagara

Archbishop Lynch of Toronto, in the pastoral letter he issued at the opening of a monastery at Niagara Falls in 1875, described the feelings of peace and hope that he believed the Christian pilgrim would discover at Niagara:

> He looks upon that broad, deep and turbulent volume of water, dashing over a precipice . . . and thinks of the awful power of Him who speaks in "the voice of many waters," and of his own last leap into eternity. In hope he raises his eyes and sees quietly ascending clouds formed from the spray, bridged in the center by the beautiful rainbow. Again he cries out: "Let my prayer ascend as incense in Thy sight. Let my last sigh be one of love, after making my peace with God and the world."[104]

Several years earlier, Lynch had suggested to Pope Pius IX that a pilgrim shrine be established at Niagara Falls and dedicated to "Our Lady of Peace." The archbishop made this proposal at the beginning of the American Civil War, when he felt "moved with sorrow at the loss of many lives and the prospect of so many souls going before God in judgement, some it is to be feared, but ill prepared, and at the sight of the beautiful rainbow that spanned the cataract, the sign of peace between God and the sinner." Pius IX complied, dedicating the shrine in 1861 "to avail for all future time."[105]

Several other proposals to establish institutions dedicated to peace at Niagara Falls have been put forth, but none has succeeded. For example, Leonard Henkle, a successful inventor from Rochester, New York, proposed the construction in 1895 of an enormous meeting hall—averaging forty-six stories in height—to be built out into the river just above the falls. He envisioned that each nation would send representatives to this "International Hall" where all would discover their common humanity, a discovery that would eventually bring about the complete elimination of war and poverty.[106]

Henkle's idealistic scheme was not the last to go unrealized at Niagara.[107] In 1945 an international committee proposed to site the new United Nations Headquarters on Navy Island, a Canadian possession about three miles upriver from the falls. The following year, when it became clear that only American sites would be seriously considered, a similar proposal was made for an adjacent island in American territory. The promoters called Navy Island "the ideal site for the world peace capital" because, as they put it, "here there is peace." Peace was a "spiritual attribute" of the site. But it was more than this, for "here too," they pointed out, was "international peace, long established, enduring." This, they felt, made the Niagara region particularly appropriate:

> Surely, to those who will implement the purpose of the United Nations, it will be inspiring to execute their high duties in a locality steeped in traditions of peace and good-neighborliness, among peoples of various ancestry who have forged indissoluble bonds of international good will and co-operation, and who have made peace work.[108]

The international peace along the Niagara has moved many to express similar sentiments. Sir Angus Fletcher, for instance, who served as the British consul at Buffalo during World War II, once remarked: "We have won, as it were, a local victory over war."[109] These sentiments have helped to inspire at least one successful international venture: the construction and dedication of the Peace Bridge in 1927.[110]

A number of peace conferences have taken place at Niagara Falls. During the Civil War, several prominent Confederate statesmen sailed around the Union navy and up the St. Lawrence to Niagara. Horace Greeley, convinced that these Southerners wanted to sue for peace, became their self-appointed intercessor with President Lincoln. After considerable exchange of messages, Greeley convinced Lincoln in 1864 to send his personal secretary, Major John Hay, to Niagara. It seemed for a time that the two parties were close to an agreement to end the war. Greeley believed that the Confederacy was willing to agree to the abolition of slavery in exchange for some $400 million in compensation. No agreement could be reached, however, and Major Hay left Niagara quickly.[111]

Canada was the host of a second peace conference at Niagara Falls in 1914, when an incident involving the landing of American marines at Vera Cruz created international tension. Mexico was already in the midst of revolution, and it now appeared that an American invasion was imminent. The governments of Argentina, Brazil, and Chile offered to mediate the dispute. Montreal and Havana were suggested as neutral sites, but the parties eventually agreed upon Niagara Falls. After two months of negotiation, the tension between Mexico and the United States was successfully defused, although Mexico's internal strife continued.[112]

Although it is difficult to find explicit connections between these peace conferences and the view of death as "Eternal Rest and Happiness," it seems safe to posit an indirect link. The first official recognition of Niagara Falls as a place of peace—the shrine to Our Lady of Peace—was indeed inspired by such a vision of death. Archbishop Lynch tied his proposal to a symbolic interpretation of individual experience at the falls. The success of this proposal, along with the dissemination of travelers' accounts which described the falls as a peaceful spectacle, helped to create a tradition of associating Niagara with peace—which in turn made it an appropriate site for a peace conference.

Peace at Niagara has nearly always been connected with prior violence. This peace is not the absence of wrath but its aftermath. The rainbow arrives after the fury of the flood has spent itself. The bliss of heaven follows the purifying hell of the abyss. The Christian can conceive of the afterlife as peaceful only because Christ, in James K. Liston's words,

> Endures the Father's curse and braves the storm
> Which threaten'd on our guilty heads to burst,
> And leave us deluged everlastingly
> Below the surges of a sea of wrath.[113]

And in the opinion of John Dowling, a Providence minister who visited in the 1840s, the Christian could interpret the rainbow as a sign of peace only for that same reason:

> That overwhelming cataract of wrath,
> Which on my Savior pour'd to rescue me
> Thus may I gaze upon the bow of mercy.[114]

Even the peace that Archbishop Lynch had in mind when he proposed the peace shrine had this connection with divine wrath. Lynch felt that Niagara Falls itself would inspire people to seek an alternative to this wrath:

> In this holy retreat of Niagara Falls many will find the road to heaven, and the true pleasure of serving God, and the real joy of having escaped the terrors of the world to come.[115]

Moreover, comparing Niagara Falls to an altar, even one with a foamy white altarcloth, has its own violent implications. An altar, after all, is a place of sacrifice; the altar that Noah built after the flood was a place of blood sacrifice. Lynch proposed the peace shrine at Niagara after blood had been spilled in the Civil War. Similarly, the peace conferences in 1864 and 1914 were prompted by prior bloodshed. The United Nations proposals came in response to the massive destruction of the Second World War.

The oft-noted peace along the Niagara Frontier that helped to inspire the United Nations' proposals and the dedication of the Peace Bridge is actually a recent development. Like the rainbow after the deluge, it is a peace that follows a great deal of bloodshed. Conflict on the Niagara may be due in part to its geographical situation as a point of narrow separation along the natural barrier of the Great Lakes. Even before Europeans arrived, this was a place of conflict between the Iroquois who lived south of the lakes and the Hurons who lived to the north.[116] Later, Niagara became the scene of a series of bloody battles between the British and the French, culminating with a British victory in 1759.[117] The worst violence along this river came in the conflict of 1812–14. Indeed, Niagara was the only continuous theater of battle during this period. Every major settlement on both sides of the river was destroyed. In the Battle of Lundy's Lane alone—fought within earshot of the falls—nearly 2,000 perished.[118] Although this was the last declared war on the Niagara frontier, open conflict was to flare up twice more. During the Canadian rebellion of 1837, the Upper Canadian rebels—abetted by American sympathizers—set up camp on Navy Island and prepared to invade Canada. International tension reached a peak in 1838 when a Canadian force crossed to the American shore, burned a steamship which had been ferrying supplies to the rebels, and sent it drifting toward the falls. Support for the rebel cause gradually diminished in part because the United States government repeatedly stated its neutrality.[119] Finally, in 1866, 1,500 members of the Fenian Brotherhood crossed the Niagara River intending, through the conquest of Canada, to force Britain to free Ireland. In a disorganized series of bloody clashes, the invaders were eventually repulsed. Only after this point can we say that real peace came to the Niagara Frontier.[120]

It was this history of violence that the British statesman and former member of parliament Lord Morpeth had in mind when he composed these lines in 1841:

> Oh! may the waves which madden in thy deep
> *There* spend their rage nor climb the encircling steep;
> And till the conflict of thy surges cease
> The nations on thy banks repose in peace.[121]

Nearly all the images of peace at Niagara are, like this one, images of spent fury. Paradoxically, then, Niagara may have become a symbol of peace precisely because it had been the scene of so much violence, human and natural.

The nature of the possible worlds beyond death's door, so elaborately described at Niagara Falls, may seem simply irrelevant to many of us today, but in the nineteenth century, death obviously had more salience. An increasing emphasis on the individual as a subject with unique experiences and as a competitive economic actor, particularly among the growing ranks of the middle class, may have increased concern with death, the ultimate individual experience. The meaning of death was being negotiated, partly in response to the impact of Darwinism and other critiques of conventional religious beliefs. Some of Niagara's visitors questioned the traditional Christian view of death. But the idea that there might be no sequel to death—be it heaven, limbo, purgatory, or hell—was still uncommon. Those who wrote about death at Niagara assumed an afterlife, and the possibilities of its nature fascinated them, not just because each believed he or she would one day experience it, but also because exercising one's imagination in this way was exhilarating. The opaque face of death, and indeed the landscape of Niagara Falls itself, was a screen on which they could project their deepest fears and their highest aspirations. But Niagara's landscape was not completely opaque: it had a certain structure which could be interpreted in a way that fit the prevailing Christian understanding of death. Those who articulated the metaphorical meaning of Niagara's landscape often produced written texts. In addition, certain behavior patterns, traditions, and elements of the human landscape at Niagara also form a series of texts that further articulate both the landscape's metaphorical meaning and, indeed, the meanings of death itself.

four

THE NATURE OF NIAGARA

*T*hroughout the nineteenth century and well into the twentieth, travelers described Niagara Falls as nature's highest expression. The falls, in their eyes, was more than just a *part* of nature, it was nature's "visible symbol,"[1] "Nature's loudest voice,"[2] "Nature's holiest temple."[3] James Dixon, a Connecticut writer and politician, wrote in 1848 that it was "as if nature had sat in council with herself to create a living embodiment of her utmost power, sovereign glory, irresistible force, rapid motion."[4] It is certainly less surprising that visitors should see Niagara Falls as the "visible symbol" of nature than that they should see it as a symbol of death or the future. People came to Niagara, first and foremost, to experience nature. Nature is the most fundamental of the four themes explored in this book. In a sense it underlies the others and hence is important, at least implicitly, in every chapter.

Those who wrote about nature at Niagara were more often than not participants in a larger nineteenth-century dialogue about the meaning of nature in light of new knowledge and power. Most visitors arrived at the falls with certain conceptions and prejudices about the natural world. Among these conceptions is the idea, expressed again and again, that nature attracts us because it is mysterious, somehow inaccessible. In his famous essay, *Nature,* Emerson describes nature as "all that is separate from us":

> The stars awaken a certain reverence because though always present, they are always inaccessible; but all natural objects make a similar impression. . . . Neither does the wisest man extort all her secret and lose his curiosity by finding out all her perfection.[5]

Although one could stand within inches of Niagara Falls, for many visitors it was similarly impenetrable. The famous British traveler Mrs. Frances Trollope, who found little to impress her in America, put it this way in 1832: "There is a shadowy mystery hangs about it which neither the eye nor even the imagination can penetrate."[6] The anonymous author of *Legend of the Whirl-pool* (1840) expressed the same idea in verse: "Strange myst'ries bide beneath the waves, and man, / Hath yet to know a thousand things that nature hides."[7] This author went on to explain just why the sense of the unknown in natural objects is so attractive: "Indeed, in this, mainly consists the secret fascination and charm, that so attracts us to scenes of wonder and sublimity. They bring forth unusual emotions of the mind, and turn it from its wonted channel. They abstract us from our daily and ordinary duties, and as in a vision, for a period transport us to a new world."

From this perspective, nature's otherness—its separateness from us—renders it mysterious, like a new world. Thus Niagara, which many saw as an embodiment of nature's otherness, needed to be kept separate from encroaching settlement. This sentiment provided much of the impetus for the establishment of parks surrounding the falls. Recall James C. Carter's words at the dedication of the American Reservation: the state of New York marks "the boundaries of the sanctuary, [and] expels from the interior all ordinary human pursuits and claims."[8] One experience of nature's otherness, then, is to feel oneself transported to a mysterious new world, a sanctuary.

Others have expressed the otherness of nature in more disturbing terms. Northrop Frye proposes that we naturally think of nature as "otherness, the sense of something not ourselves," but this otherness is not merely a physical counterpart to our consciousness: "For the imagination it is rather some kind of force or power or will that is not ourselves, an otherness of spirit."[9] Frye's comment is relevant to much that has been written about nature at Niagara, where nature is powerful and active. To repeat James Dixon's words, Niagara is "a living embodiment of [nature's] utmost power, sovereign glory, irresistible force, rapid motion." Many travelers experienced the cataract as a terrifying, almost alien presence that seemed completely indifferent to human concerns.

Trying to make sense of natural objects that combine beauty and darkness, that inspire both fear and exaltation, led to the idea of the natural sublime, a development I touched on in Chapter 1. The rhetoric of the natural sublime gave visitors a way both to comprehend and to express their responses to Niagara Falls. In Kant's view, the key element of the sublime was not the overwhelming natural object itself, but the awareness it evoked in the viewer of the human capacity to expand and measure oneself as equal to it. Consider this 1843 account from James Silk Buckingham, an English travel writer who visited nearly every corner of the empire:

> How humble, then, are we, who stand thus overwhelmed and overawed by such an inconsiderable fragment of the great whole as this, before which we seem but as dust in the balance? Yet, at the same time, "how fearfully and wonderfully are we made," when, amidst all this grandeur, of which the human intellect and the immortal spirit form so important a part, we seem blind to the dignity with which we are invested—as the living, feeling, thinking, reflecting, reasoning, and hoping inhabitants and possessors of such a world as our domain![10]

The sort of reflexivity Buckingham expresses was central to romantic depictions of the human encounter with nature. "In the tranquil landscape," writes Emerson, "and especially in the distant line of the horizon, man beholds somewhat as beautiful as his own nature."[11] The evidence at Niagara suggests that the vision of human nature reflected in the mirror of nature also has a dark as well as a beautiful side.

Perhaps the element most basic to the nineteenth-century fascination with nature is the idea that nature is a realm separate from the ordinary world: it is other. Because of this separateness, this inaccessibility, nature could be imagined as containing possibilities unknown in the world of daily experience. Hence the sublime natural object could attain a quasi-religious power. To conceive of Niagara Falls as a symbol and embodiment of nature, therefore, was not unlike—indeed, could reinforce—seeing the falls through the veil of distance or envisioning the possibilities of the afterlife. Certainly other conceptions of nature coexisted with this one; since the Enlightenment, for example, some had depicted nature as a vast mechanism. But for our purposes here, we will focus on the otherness of nature. If nature is somehow inaccessible to us, its content and character are visible only in imagination. We can then ask how those who came to Niagara imagined nature. Leo Marx has suggested that *Moby Dick* can be interpreted as "an exploration of the nature of nature."[12] Written and nonwritten responses to nature at Niagara comprise a similar exploration of the nature of nature. The resulting picture of nature's nature coalesces into several pairs of contrasting images. The following pages will examine these images, beginning with the most distant—those that depict a primordial natural world predating human consciousness—and concluding with the most intimate—those that reflexively explore the nature of human nature. Although it will be necessary for the purposes of analysis to describe each half of the pairs of contrasting images separately, it is important to keep in mind that the power of the sublime comes from the tension between the two.

How have travelers imagined nature at Niagara Falls? One way has been to interpret nature's remoteness temporally. Part of Niagara's appeal is that, as a recent Lebanese visitor has put it, it is "a mystery with a hidden past."[13] The falls emerge "out of the far off past" in an 1886 poem by the Buffalo librarian and writer James Warner Ward, its antiquity carved in stone:

> ... many a voiceless century
> Into the shadow past had vanished recordless,
>   Did not the lines and chinks of thy shrewd chiselling,
> Scarring the polished tablets of thy centotaph,
>   Tell us the mystic story of thy genesis.[14]

Because nature predates the human world, to encounter nature is, in a sense, to encounter the past. While gazing at Niagara Falls, many nineteenth- and early twentieth-century visitors imagined a primordial world where nature reigned, undisturbed by the intrusion of human will. Niagara was a survivor and hence a representative vestige of that world. The remoteness of the primordial world left its character open to speculation. The experience of encountering the primordial world was personal, but the speculations that emerged, like the images of the afterlife examined in the last chapter, were informed by contemporary scientific and especially religious ideas.

When Niagara's visitors began to depict the prehuman world, their descriptions had two common features. First, they all agreed that the world of primordial nature was radically different from our own, and second, they saw that primordial world in polarized terms: it was either terrible or beautiful, a world of chaos or a Garden of Eden. For the sake of clarity, we will consider these positive and negative—the light and dark—depictions separately, although it should be noted that some visitors were themselves ambivalent about the prehuman world. The fascination with any remote realm rests on the extremely divergent characteristics it may possibly contain. Death would hold little appeal for imagination if all souls were assured of paradise.

Positive descriptions of the prehuman world took several forms in the literature of Niagara Falls. Some visitors depicted nature as joyous and innocent from the very beginning. James Silk Buckingham, for instance, described Niagara's origin with these lines in 1838:

> Thy reign is of the ancient days, thy sceptre from on high,
> Thy birth was when the morning stars together sang with joy.[15]

In a poem about Niagara's sound, the early twentieth-century scholar and poet, Katherine Lee Bates, asked:

> Do your tremendous paeans still prolong
> Creation's old, unhumanised delight,
> The laughter of the Titans?[16]

These writers imagined the time before humans appeared as one of pristine innocence and delight, and they imagined Niagara as a representative from that era.

Other writers saw the purity of the prehuman world as a result of a previous victory over original chaos. An anonymous poem that appeared in P. A. Porter's *Goat Island* (1900) exemplifies this view. (If this were a purely literary study, verse of this sort, produced by the common amateur would surely be ignored. But our concern for the explication of widespread beliefs and ideas means that we must bring all classes of writing within our ken.) The poem begins by asking the "Great Fall": "Canst thou unveil / The secrets of thy birth?" Niagara's answer reveals that its birth came after the Creator's pronouncement, "Let there be light":

> When I was born
> The stars of morn
> Together sang—'twas day:
> The sun unrolled
> His garb of gold
> And took his upward way.

In the next stanza, we find that the young world was beautiful and pure:

> He mounted high
> The eastern sky
> And then looked down to earth;
> And she was there,
> Young, fresh, and fair,
> And I, and all, had birth.

But then we learn that this purity was the fruit of a triumph over "dark chaos":

The word of power
Was spoke that hour:
Dark chaos felt the shock;
Forth sprung the light,
Burst day from night
Up leaped the living rock.[17]

Niagara was part of a fresh and beautiful natural world established by the Creator's victory over chaos. This pure world, uncorrupted as yet by human defiance, mirrored the Creator's goodness.

Many visitors explicitly compared Niagara to the earthly paradise. Playing off this notion, Mark Twain's satirical tale, *Extracts from Adam's Diary,* placed Niagara Falls at the center of the Garden of Eden. "The great waterfall," Adam writes in his diary, "is the finest thing on the estate."[18] But Eve soon brings trouble to paradise with her plan to make it into a "tidy summer resort." She begins by putting up signs saying "KEEP OFF THE GRASS" and "CAVE OF THE WINDS THIS WAY,"[19] and ends by introducing death to the world.

In a more solemn tone, Richard Lewis Johnson, an early preservationist and editor of a guidebook on Niagara Falls, wondered how Eden could have lacked a Niagara. In his "Apostrophe to Niagara" (1898), an exploration of the cataract's past, Johnson could see that Niagara was ancient; the gorge had been cut by "ante-glacial flood," and could be followed back to Niagara's beginning in the "Primeval dawn." Finally, on Goat Island which sits atop the escarpment between the two waterfalls, Johnson found paradise itself:

For the lost Eden, search no more,
In myth or prehistoric lore;
That question's settled, ever more
On this Sacred Isle.

Whose ferns and mosses scent the breeze,
Where east and west each soul agrees,
The Tigris and the Euphrates
Flow swiftly, gladly on.[20]

The Tigris and the Euphrates are, of course, the two branches of the upper Niagara River.

Many visitors have echoed Johnson's suggestion that Goat Island might be the "lost Eden." John Montclair's "Niagara" (1865), for instance, describes Goat Island in similar language:

> A fairy isle trembles on the cataract's crest,
> Beloved by the waves, that hold it compressed;
> And, like worshipping Magii, rainbows arise,
> 'Neath these acres of paradise dropped from the skies.[21]

These travelers, of course, were certainly not the first to imagine paradise (or utopia) as an island. The isolation of Goat Island enhanced its appeal. One had to cross seething rapids to reach it, and until the first bridge was built in 1817, it was totally inaccessible.[22] In 1854 the young English traveler Isabella Lucy Bird, who would one day be the first woman admitted to the Royal Geographical Society, found "everything of terrestrial beauty" on Goat Island. She accounted for its charm in this way: "It stands amid the eternal din of the waters, a barrier between the Canadian and American Falls. It is not more than sixty-two acres in extent, yet it has groves of huge forest trees, and secluded roads underneath them in the deepest shade, far apparently from the busy world, yet thousands from every part of the globe yearly tread its walks of beauty."[23] In 1870, William Barham—an English writer who edited a book of poems and descriptions of Niagara Falls—arrived at the same conclusion: "Situated in the midst of the rapids, and surrounded by them on three sides, this island is one of the most beautiful, fascinating and romantic places in the world; it affords a delightful retreat for 'the lunatic, the lover and the poet,' to indulge in their meditations." Barham felt a reluctance on leaving Goat Island and was reminded of a passage in Milton where Eve asks:

> Must I leave thee, Paradise?
> —Those happy walks and shades,
> Fit haunt of gods?[24]

Goat Island's physical remoteness helped these visitors to imagine it as the temporally remote Eden. In all of the descriptions we have considered so far, Niagara Falls (or the island embedded within it) was a representative or a survivor from a fresh and beautiful prehuman world. Both Niagara and the primordial world it represented could be pictured in ideal terms because of their imagined remoteness from the humanized world of the present.

Those who wrote dark descriptions of primordial nature often identified Niagara with the forces of chaos. In "The Genius of Niagara" (1869), by Buffalo minister John C. Lord, Niagara's chaos is older then creation itself:

> Emblem of power—the mighty Sun
>   Hath found and left thee roaring on,
> Thou wert with Chaos, e'er his light
>   Shone out upon the starless night,
> Sole relic of that awful day
> When all in wild confusion lay.[25]

An earlier poem by the prolific if sentimental New Englander, Mrs. Lydia Huntley Sigourney, suggests that chaos was not completely conquered by the Creator's work and still wrestles against the powers of light:

> Creep stealthily, and snatch a trembling glance
> Into the dread abyss.
>   What there thou seest
> Shall dwell forever in thy secret soul,
> Finding no form of language.
>   The vexed deep,
> Which from the hour that Chaos heard the voice
> "Let there be light," hath known no pause or rest.[26]

Many of Niagara's visitors associated ancient nature with the biblical flood, wherein the Creator released the forces of chaos to destroy the human world. The following stanza from "Niagara" (1847), by the Rhode Island writer Henry Howard Brownell, conveys this sense of reappearing chaos:

> Has aught like this descended since the fountains
> Of the Great Deep, broke up, in cataracts hurled,

And climbed lofty hills, eternal mountains,
Poured wave on wave above a buried world?[27]

To relate Niagara to the biblical deluge is to mark it as humanity's foe, but it is also to give it a certain awesome appeal.
Consider these lines from "Niagara" (1884), by the Scottish aris-
tocrat and governor-general of Canada, John Douglas Southerland, the marquis of Lorne:

So poured the avenging streams upon the world
When swung the ark upon the deluge wave,
And o'er each precipice in grandeur hurled,
The endless torrents gave mankind a grave.[28]

To see this ancient event in Niagara is to place the waterfall on a
vast and distant stage where words like "endless" and "grandeur"
can resound in the fullness of imaginative reverie.

Visitors often described Niagara as an eternal force, un-
changed since the dawn of time. The prehuman world that
Niagara represented, whether viewed positively or negatively,
was a natural world. But nature's deep extension into the past was
only part of its appeal to imagination.

At Niagara a second pair of contrasting images depict nature's
distance from the human world, its otherness, but without reference to time.

In the first vision, nature is a life-giving fountain. Viewing
sublime natural objects helps sustain us because, as one mid-
nineteenth-century visitor wrote of the falls, we are invited to
"drink deep of the spacious fountain which she slivers over."[29] In
"Niagara" (1867), by the American poet John Edward Howell,
the fountain of nature renews us because it is none other than the
Fountain of Youth:

Fountain of Youth, and sovereign symbol, too
Let him who thirsts drink deeply of thy wave—
Feel as his cheek renews its summer hue,
Baptismal blessings on his brow, . . .[30]

Such statements are more than verbal images: visitors claimed
that they actually experienced nature at Niagara as a life-giving

force. The prominent Swedish novelist Fredrika Bremer, who visited the falls in 1850, expressed the texture of this experience very clearly when she wrote: ". . . the water here has the most delightful freshness, that I can compare to nothing with which I am acquainted. But it feels to me like the spirit of a delicious, immortal youth. Yes, here it seems to me as if one might become young again in body and in soul." And as she took her last look at Niagara, she found that her initial impression endured: "The green colour of the water, its expressively delightful, living odour, charms me as much as ever. I shall always, in recalling it, think of the fountains of eternal youth."[31] Although Niagara is harmless in these descriptions, we note that it is still enormously powerful, for it is indeed a potent thing that can deliver "eternal youth."

A second vision of nature's otherness contrasts sharply with these luminous images of Niagara Falls. In positive images, nature's distance from the human world, its otherness, consists in the fact that it is pure and unfallen while the human world is afflicted with corruption and death. In this second vision, the otherness of nature takes a more unsettling form. The narrator of William Dean Howell's *Their Wedding Journey* (1888) captures this quality of otherness in a passage near the end of the novel:

> We come to Niagara in the patronizing spirit in which we approach everything nowadays. . . . But after a while we are aware of some potent influence undermining our self-satisfaction; we begin to conjecture that the great cataract does not exist by virtue of our approval, and to feel that it will not cease when we go away. The second day makes us its abject slaves, and on the third we want to flee from it in terror.[32]

Similarly, Francis Lieber, a German scholar and editor who visited the falls in the early 1830s, writes: "From the moment when you first see Niagara, to the hour when you leave it, one of the great Characteristics with which it strikes the soul of man, is that, like the sea or the Alps, it does and will exist without him."[33] It is not the mere fact that nature can go on without us that makes it terrifying. Rather, as other writers have pointed out explicitly, it is that the chaos of the primordial world lives on in nature. This is Ishmael's message in the fifty-eighth chapter of *Moby Dick*:

"Foolish mortals, Noah's flood is not yet subsided: two-thirds of the fair world it yet covers. . . . No mercy, no power but its own controls it. Panting and snorting like a mad battle steed that has lost its rider, the masterless ocean overruns the globe."[34] Similarly, Niagara, in the words of various visitors, is "a gigantic, pitiless force, a blind passion of nature, uncontrolled and uncontrollable," "a fiend, ever fierce for new victims," a "Proud Demon of the waters," whose power is "pitiless, remorseless, resistless, like that of a volcano or a tornado."[35]

Yet a power this inhuman can only appear as a great mystery; despite the danger, it can arouse our curiosity. Charles Dudley Warner, the Connecticut writer and newspaper editor, in this passage from his novel, *Their Pilgrimage* (1897), captures the compelling grandeur of Niagara's inhuman side: "In this unknown, which was rather felt than seen, there was a sense of power and of mystery which overcame the mind; and in the black night the roar, the cruel haste of the rapids, tossing white gleams and hurrying to the fatal plunge, begat a sort of terror in the spectators. It was a power implacable, vengeful, not to be measured."[36]

Corresponding to these two visions of nature's otherness, visitors expressed contrasting responses to Niagara Falls itself. In immediate response to the vision of nature as a pitiless flood, individuals usually were inspired by a frantic desire to protect themselves by taking action. Another description of Niagara from Warner's novel provides a typical example of this reaction: "Shut the windows and lock the door, you could not shut the terror of it. The town did not seem safe; the bridges, the buildings at the edge of the precipices with their shaking casements, the islands, might at any moment be engulfed and disappear. It was a thing to flee from."[37] But flight is not the only possible form of action; one can also presume to fight back. Alfred Domett, an English traveler and poet who would one day become prime minister of New Zealand, observed in the early 1830s, that it is because you must "confess the scene almost overpowering and cannot without some effort preserve your self-command," and because "the thick mist flying in your face . . . brings you, as it were, almost in the power of the terrific element," that Niagara is "a scene for the Prometheus-like defier of the power of matter wielded by omnipotence to try his courage in, to fancy his strength of resolution and resistance tested there."[38] In this sense even a pitiless force can be valuable, for it provides the opportunity to exercise one's Promethean urges.

The typical response inspired by the vision of nature as a fountain was to do nothing, to acquiesce. One only had to bathe in the presence of this fountain and to calmly accept transport to a world that was pure, beautiful, and eternal. A passage from Anthony Trollope's *North America* (1862), as already quoted in chapter 2, accurately expresses this view:

> To realize Niagara, *you must sit there* [my emphasis] till you see nothing else than that which you have come to see. You will hear nothing else. At length you will be at one with the tumbling river before you. You will find yourself among the waters as though you belonged to them. The cool, liquid green will run through your veins, and the voice of the cataract will be the expression of your own heart. You will fall as the bright waters fall, rushing down into your new world with no hesitation and no dismay; and you will rise again as the spray rises, bright, beautiful and pure. Then you will flow away in your course to the uncompassed, distant, and eternal ocean.[39]

Trollope's reaction to Niagara bears comparison to that of Harriet Beecher Stowe who wrote: "I felt as if I could have gone over with the waters; it would have been so beautiful a death; there would be no fear in it."[40] Although neither Stowe nor Trollope actually responded to Niagara with action, we have seen that many people did jump into the river, some after expressing sentiments such as theirs. Trollope's urge to merge himself with eternal nature, to "be at one with the tumbling river," and Stowe's longing for a "beautiful" death with "no fear in it" share with the suicide's motivation a desire to escape this world; but instead of annihilating themselves, they simply want to lose themselves in another world.

There is also a connection between death and negative images of nature. A pitiless force is terrifying, in part, because potentially it can kill. William Fleming, a romantically inclined English physician, expressed exactly this fear in 1835 when he wrote: "I never listened to the sound of Niagara without the impression that an inexhaustible power was in action, which, unless restrained and subdued, must instantly annihilate me."[41]

Perhaps images of nature mirror images of death at Niagara because both nature and death highlight the boundaries of the human world. But while they both reveal human limitedness, they also hold forth the promise of something beyond—a realm where, in imagination at least, we can transcend our limits.

So far we have looked at immediate responses to nature at Niagara, that is, at how individuals felt while gazing at the falls itself. Many visitors also expressed their views of nature by responding to Niagara's built landscape—the towers and bridges, the factories, the two cities. Light and dark visions of nature would seem to imply two complementary visions of the world humans have made and, therefore, two views of how humans should relate to nature. If nature is joyous and innocent, the world that humans displace it with is, by implication, evil and contaminated. James K. Liston, a poet from western Upper Canada, in his "Niagara Falls: A Poem in Three Cantos" (1843), wrote: "Thus, was the Fall of Man a foul, uncouth / Abrupt declension."[42] The human world is the product of a fall from a world that was pure. In contrast, if nature is a vengeful, remorseless power, then the human world is the result of a triumph over chaos and darkness. It is a realm of order and freedom. The fall is not a fall at all but, as Lucifer's name implies, an enlightenment. These two views of the human world—that it is either a triumph over chaos or a fall from natural purity—correspond to two equally contrasting evaluations of Niagara's human landscape. If Niagara Falls was nature's "living symbol," one could observe there, in microcosm, the relation between nature and the human world. Let us begin by examining some critical responses to Niagara's human landscape.

The young Englishwoman Isabella Lucy Bird, who visited Niagara Falls in 1854, directed her comments first to the American side, where she saw "an enormous wooden many-windowed fabric, said to be the largest paper-mill in the United States. A whole collection of mills disfigures this romantic spot." On the British side she found something equally unattractive: "a great fungus growth of museums, curiosity-shops, taverns, and pagodas with shining tin cupolas."[43] Venders and hawkers pestered the English traveler W. G. Marshall during his stay at Niagara in 1881, but the condition of the landscape bothered him more: "But worse, far worse than these annoyances is the wholesale, ruthless destruction of the natural beauty of the gorge. Trees, aye, forests have been cut down to make room for unsightly factories, for hotels, museums, drinking saloons and what not."[44]

R. E. Garczynski's evaluation of Niagara's built landscape, which appeared in William Cullen Bryant's popular illustrated volume, *Picturesque America* (1872), is perhaps the most damning:

> All its approaches are plain, dull and tedious. The country around is ... dotted with white-painted wooden houses, ugly churches, homely factories, and mills. . . . The villages that now crowd around its vicinity have no recommendations on the score of fine taste; and, though the numbers that resort hither from every land have made large hotels necessary, it has never been thought worth while to surround them with gardens, or to do aught that should remove the utilitarian look of the place. Niagara, it must be confessed, resembles a superb diamond set in lead. The stone is perfect, but the setting is lamentably vile and destitute of beauty.[45]

Anthony Trollope—who, you will recall, wanted to become "at one with the tumbling river"—found the buildings at the falls uniformly "tasteless." He would have preferred a pure Niagara without "edifices of this description which cry aloud to the gods by the force of their own ugliness and malposition. As to such," he concluded, "it might be said that there should somewhere exist a power capable of crushing them at their birth."[46]

Some visitors expressed a more positive view of the human landscape at Niagara. The small steamboat, *Maid of the Mist,* which carried tourists to the foot of the falls, inspired George William Curtis to offer this tribute to human daring in 1852:

There we tremble, in perfect security, mocking with our little Maid the might of Niagara. For Man is the magician, and as he plants his foot upon the neck of mountains, and passes the awful Alps, safely as the Israelites through the divided sea, so he dips his hand into Niagara, and gathering a few drops from it waters, educes a force from Niagara itself, by which he confronts and defies it.[47]

Nearly all descriptions of Niagara's bridges have also been positive. Evelyn Watson, a Buffalo writer who composed more than fifty poems on Niagara Falls and its surroundings, wrote these lines in 1929:

The chasms of nature seem wide but nation and nation
Shall find in this river a bond, and not separation—
Men are the forgers of bridges.[48]

It is not surprising that ships and bridges should be appealing; their forms and their functions are clear, necessary, and often aesthetically pleasant. But it is surprising that mills and power plants should also be seen this way.

Evelyn Watson, who seemed to take pride in the rapid industrialization of her region, described an early hydroelectric plant as:

a citadel of light,
That sends across the state a living shower
Of stars, as lamps, as "hands," as lightened labor.[49]

James K. Liston had a similar response to the paper mills that crowded Goat Island in the 1840s:

In the Foam-Girt Isle
Are Mills, wherein, transformed, the useless rag
Becomes a vehicle of human thought
Conveyed thereby to Earth's remotest bounds.[50]

A final example comes from Edward Zaremba's "Niagara Captive" (1913). This poem admonishes the "red men" for letting Niagara's power go to waste, and concludes with this celebration of human power over nature:

'Tis to the people do we dedicate
The Wonders of Today.[51]

It is tempting to interpret some actual landscape features at
Niagara as responses to nature. Is there a direct connection, for
example, between the factories, mills, and power plants and the
view that nature is a chaotic force that must be conquered?
Interpretation would be simple if the urge to develop Niagara
were equated with the vision of nature as a pitiless flood, and if
the urge to preserve it were equated with the vision of nature as a
life-giving fountain. Unfortunately, things are not this simple.
The ironic connection between images of nature at Niagara and
its industrial and economic development is the subject of the next
chapter. Here, it will suffice to show that the urge to preserve
Niagara—an urge that has had tangible effects on the
landscape—has been associated with quite divergent images of
nature.

As we have seen, in the 1880s, New York State and the
Province of Ontario created small parks at Niagara Falls. This
was in response to a rising tide of public concern about the desecration of this natural "sanctuary," as James C. Carter called it at
the dedication of the American reservation.[52] We have already
been exposed to several complaints about the ugliness and inap-
propriateness of the built landscape at Niagara. These seemed to
be attacks on the human world *per se*. They were based on a
vision of Niagara as an emblem of natural purity and beauty, and
on a concomitant fear that Niagara might be contaminated. But
there was another reason for wanting to isolate Niagara from the
human world: to preserve not its beauty, but its mystery.

The narrator of Howells's *Their Wedding Journey,* who wanted
to flee from the falls in terror when he realized that "the great
cataract does not exist by virtue of our approval," also wanted to
preserve it from too much human interference. His motivation, it
seems, was an appreciation of the dark side of nature's otherness:

> The place is inexpressibly lonely and dreadful, and one feels
> like an alien presence there, or as if he had intruded upon
> some mood or haunt of nature in which she had a right to be

forever alone. The slight impudent structure of the elevator rises through the solitude like a thing that merits ruin, yet it is better than something more elaborate, for it looks temporary, and since there must be an elevator, it is well to have it of the most transitory aspect.[53]

Those who felt a merciless power at Niagara did not necessarily feel an urge to subdue it. In 1839 the British romanticist and scholar, Mrs. Anna B. Jameson, wrote that this power gave her "a sensation of rapturous terror." "The idea, too," she continued, "of the immediate danger, the consciousness that any thing caught within its verge is inevitably hurried to a swift destination, swallowed up, annihilated, thrills of blood." For Mrs. Jameson, the intrusions of humanity offended not the purity but the majesty of nature. She wrote:

> The Americans have disfigured their share of the rapids with mills and manufactories, and horrid red brick houses, and other unacceptable, unseasonable sights and signs of sordid industry. Worse than all is the round tower, which some profane wretch has erected on the Cresent Fall. . . . I do hope the violated majesty of nature will take the matter in hand, and overwhelm or cast it down the precipice one of these fine days. . . .[54]

Although the parks of the 1880s protected the immediate vicinity of the falls from encroachment by mills, curiosity shops, and the like, they failed to protect Niagara from another form of human interference: hydroelectric development. As the twentieth century progressed, the development of hydroelectric power claimed a greater and greater amount of water, until today almost seventy percent of Niagara's yearly flow is diverted for power generation. For those attracted to the falls for its beauty, perhaps this is not a great loss. But for those seeking its terrible power, this is the most insidious form of intervention.

In Niagara's falling waters, many visitors perceived not only nature but also human nature. Yet, this perception was hardly unique to Niagara Falls. Ishmael, the narrator of *Moby Dick,* theorizes extensively on the connection between nature and human nature. Leo Marx offers the following analysis:

Continuing his attempt to account for the fascination exercised upon mankind by the ocean, Ishmael has proposed that water is the telltale element in our relation with visible nature.... He singles out water for its "magical" properties: at times transparent, at others a mirror, water bemuses us with the possibility of penetrating the surface of nature, yet it flatters and disturbs us by casting back our own image. What do we really see—the object or ourselves?[55]

The experience of many of Niagara's visitors would seem to confirm Ishmael's theory. Evelyn Watson, for example, felt that "Poet-Nature calls to Poet-Man" and urges him to seek, in the "Inner Vista, the End, for which we yearn."[56] It was as if these visitors, to use Ishmael's image, hoped to penetrate the surface of nature in order also to penetrate the surface of human nature. Clearly they expected to find beneath that surface an "Inner Vista" that was vast and uncharted, a mysterious otherness like nature's own. The very idea of an unknown area of human nature would not have occurred to these visitors had they been viewing Niagara before the late-eighteenth century. Nor would they have considered this "Inner Vista" appealing. For, as Arnold Hauser has written, the romantics were the first to feel "the irresistible urge to introspection . . . and the compulsion to consider oneself over and over again as one unknown, as an uncannily remote stranger." Hauser argues that the romantic artist's attraction to the "remote stranger" within was part of a characteristic desire to flee reality. In this flight, the romantic "discovers that 'two souls dwell in his breast,' that something inside him feels and thinks that is not identical with himself, that he carries his demon and his judge about with him—in brief, he discovers the basic facts of psychoanalysis."[57]

The English literary critic F. L. Lucas, in a discussion of the distinction between romanticism and realism, observes that there are several ways to respond to "the preconscious and instinctive side of personality." He writes: "In each of us lies this dark lake from which our conscious, reasoning selves have gradually emerged. . . . Some of us love to dream on the banks of this mysterious mere; some try to fish or dive in it; others labour to brick it over and blot it out. . . ."[58] Many of Niagara's visitors identified the preconscious and instinctive side of personality with nature. And like external nature, they saw this nature within as indifferent to the conscious will. The range of responses that Lucas describes can all be found at Niagara.

It is important to remember that speaking of "the unconscious" is very much like speaking of heaven or hell. As the novelist D. M. Thomas has recently suggested, psychoanalysis is a modern example of mythology.[59] Freud was the discoverer, or at least the principal synthesizer of the myth. This does not mean that his theories lack an empirical foundation, but simply that they extend beyond facts to tell a story about a realm whose very existence must be postulated.

At Niagara we find two descriptions of this unknown within. In each, the hidden side of human nature is the natural side, the part that is remote from our conscious, willing selves. In the first form, the unconscious is an uncorrupted, preconscious spiritual essence, a soul. The second form identifies the unconscious side of personality with the passions—the instinctive, animal part of our nature. This is the final and most intimate pair of contrasting images of nature that I will explore in this chapter.

The sight of Niagara Falls inspired many visitors to think of the "soul": the "supernatural element," in James C. Carter's words, "in virtue of which [man] aspires to lay hold of the Infinites by which he is surrounded." This is "the highest, the profoundest element in man's nature," and, Carter continued, "its possession is what most distinguishes him from other creatures."[60] The American painter Thomas Cole found great beauty in Niagara's "green glancing depths" and in its "white misty showers," and then he proclaimed, "The soul is full of thee."[61] How can the soul resemble nature? Clearly, if nature is primordial chaos, it cannot. But if nature is pure and beautiful, if it is God's first creation which—unlike his last—never rebelled, then nature's resemblance to the soul begins to make sense. If we are born uncorrupted, then the rise to consciousness is a fall from innocent spirituality. It is thus possible to believe that the soul has not partaken in this rebellion, that it has remained unconscious, and that it yearns to lead us back to God.

An encounter with unspoiled nature—a visit to Niagara, for instance—could become for some an encounter with the unfallen part of themselves, the soul. Consider the concluding stanza from Benjamin Copeland's "Niagara" (1904):

> O mighty monitor! O seer sublime!
> The soul's surpassing grandeur thou dost show;—
>
> The fountains of thy immemorial prime
> Through man's immortal being freely flow.[62]

In this poem, the fountains of nature's youth find kinship not with our passions but with our "immortal being." Another visitor who found reflections of the unfallen soul in Niagara was the New England writer Caroline Gilman. In 1838, she wrote:

> One feels thoroughly *alone,* while overhanging that thundering mass of waters, with the silent moon treading her tranquil way. I thought of *soul,* and this mighty Fall seemed as a drop compared to the cataract of mind, which has been rushing from the bosom of the Eternal, from age to age, through every channel of human nature ... and I trust God, destined to flow in many a happy river around his throne.[63]

From this perspective, the soul emerges out of the "bosom of the Eternal" and it strives to return there. It is a part of our nature which, like nature itself, has never defied its creator.

The kind of soul described by people like Copeland and Gilman would never correspond to the unconscious as Freud conceived of it. For, in Freud's view, the unconscious was the exclusive abode of instinctual drives and repressed experiences; spirituality was simply one way to sublimate instinctual energy.[64] For Jung, on the other hand, there was a "great treasure that lies hidden in the cave of the unconscious," although we have "the feeling that it is something alien, a non-ego."[65] The treasure is the unconscious psychic center which Jung called the "self." To realize spiritual wholeness, one must strive to discover this psychic center. As we have seen, some of Niagara's visitors identified the soul with the natural part of human nature—that is, the part remote from the conscious will. I mention Jung's theory here not as an explanation of the notion that the soul is unconscious, but simply to show that the notion is not altogether novel among these visitors.

The second and more prevalent vision of the hidden or natural side of human nature corresponds with the image of external nature as a pitiless and chaotic flood. William Fleming wrote that Niagara was "an inexhaustible power ... which, unless restrained and subdued, must instantly annihilate me."[66] Other visitors felt exactly this way about the nature within them. It was an aspect of their selves they shared with animals; their human status, indeed their very survival, depended on restraining it. There were times when some felt that this inhuman force threatened to break loose at Niagara. In William Dean Howells' opinion, one of these moments came during the tightrope walk of the Great Blondin, when thousands of people gawked at this man who appeared to be gambling foolishly with his life. The appeal of the spectacle, Howells feared, rested on a secret delight in the possibility that Blondin would fall to a terrible death. Hence the show was like "the fight of a man with a wild beast." The real danger, Howells felt, was that this show "thinned the frail barrier which the aspirations of centuries had slowly erected between humanity and savagery."[67] Another event that was subject to similar criticism was the trip of the lake schooner *Michigan* over the Horseshoe Falls in 1827. Local promoters had tied a dog, two bears, a buffalo, two raccoons, and a goose on its deck. Over 15,000 spectators watched in morbid fascination as the *Michigan* took the great plunge with its cargo of "ferocious beasts."[68]

At Niagara, the force that the "frail barrier" of civilization protects us from was usually identified as passion. Many regarded Francis Abbott, the "Hermit of Niagara" whom we met earlier, as one who crossed that barrier and was then engulfed by his passions. When his body was found in the lower river, no one was sure if he had taken his own life, but his habit of hanging from a plank above the falls made him seem less than blameless. James Bird, a self-educated English shopkeeper and poet, analyzed Abbott's flaw in these lines:

Too wild for earth, too restless for the sky,
Told of the ruin passion's storm had brought,
The serpent in the Eden of his thought.[69]

Here rolls the mighty CATARACT:—but more
Of this when passion's stormy gust be o'er,
If that can ever for a moment cease:—
While sweeps the whirlwind, can we hope for peace?[70]

Here Niagara becomes a symbol for the powerful corrupt-
ing force of passion: something wild within us that must be
contained.

Because we are so easily seduced, it is difficult to keep passion
under control. Thus, some visitors used sexual imagery to describe the seductiveness of passion. Richard Watson Guilder, an
American poet and magazine editor, used Niagara's brink as a
metaphor of seductiveness in his poem "To Niagara" (1894):

Smooth, lustrous, awful, lovely curve of peril;
While far below the bending sea of beryl.

But to be lured by this "lovely curve," Gilder concluded, was to
pass the "frail barrier" that separates us from the abyss:

Pity that virgin soul on passion's brink,
Confronting fate—swift, inescapable,—
Fate, which of nature is the intent and core,
And dark and strong as the river's pour,
Cruel as love, and wild as love's first kiss!
Ah, God! the abyss.[71]

Henry Hathaway offered a similar but more elaborate treatment of this theme in his film, *Niagara* (1953).[72] In the opening
scene, Mr. Loomis (Joseph Cotten) wanders beneath the falls
wondering what its strange lure could be. He later compares it to
his attraction to his wife Rose (Marilyn Monroe). Like the river
upstream, love is gentle when it begins; but, he warns a young
woman who is staying with her husband in a nearby room, love
soon becomes impossible to resist and rushes us to destruction. In
a later scene, the young woman is directed by her husband to

move closer and closer to the falls so he can take a good picture. She stumbles, and just as it appears that she is falling, she turns and sees Rose passionately embracing another man. If the moral of the film is unclear to anyone after this scene, it becomes inescapable when Rose's husband and her lover both die beneath the pounding cataract. It is not the falls that destroys them but their own passion. The poster released with the film depicts the voluptuous Monroe sprawled seductively amid the swirling waters at Niagara's brink. The caption reads: "Marilyn Monroe and Niagara: a raging torrent of emotion that even nature can't control."[73]

Associating the destructive forces of nature with the passions is not a new idea. In fact, it is even hinted at in the Genesis account of the Flood. We have seen that many of Niagara's visitors used the Flood as a symbol of the pitiless, inhuman power of nature, but none of them ever mentioned the last part of Noah's story. After the Flood subsided and God had promised never again to release such waters, Noah immediately planted a vineyard. He then made some wine, became drunk, and "uncovered himself inside his tent." While Noah was sleeping, his youngest son, Ham, came into the tent and "saw his father's nakedness." When Ham told his two brothers what he had seen, they walked into the tent backwards to avoid seeing their father naked and covered him with a garment. Later, when Noah "learned what his youngest son had done to him," he cursed Ham and commanded him and all of his descendents to live as servants.[74] It was as if the terrifying forces of nature that had receded with the floodwaters threatened to rise again from within and could only be controlled through carefully followed rules.

The rainbow in the biblical story guaranteed that the floodwaters would never return. Some visitors felt that Niagara's rainbow also promised to calm the flood of the passions. In 1834, the British traveler and barrister Henry Tudor described the rainbow as

an angel of Hope, amid the distractions of the moral world, holding forth the bright symbol of peace and forgiveness to the sinful sons and daughters of earth, agitated, as they are, by as ceaseless a strife of rebellious passions and feelings towards their all-gracious Maker, as are the untamable waters of Niagara by the unceasing rushings of its torrent.[75]

The American visitor J. Wellsteed offered the same interpretation of Niagara's rainbow in 1849:

> I love to gaze upon the glorious bow,
> And mark the beauties of that "bridge where time,
> Of light and darkness, forms an arch sublime,"
> These wonders calm the passions of the mind.[76]

There is one way that passion has continuously and legitimately been expressed at Niagara Falls: like a "red light district," Niagara has been a great center of copulation. Since the middle of the nineteenth century, thousands of couples have come here to consummate their marriages.[77] This legitimate passion, of course, has usually been viewed as harmless and clean rather than dark and uncontrollable. Some have even related this ritualized sexual union to the image of Niagara as beautiful and uncorrupted. John Edward Howell called Niagara a "virgin priest," in this 1867 description of the pure bride's honeymoon:

> The gentle bride is half, not wholly wed;
>   Unfelt her pride of maiden innocence—
> Vows to obey, and by a wife's pure bed
>   Sanctify love, and be its own defense—
> Till at thy crystal altar, virgin priest,
>   Her nuptial pledges solemnized anew,
> She feels by thine her purity increased,
>   And journeys home a wife, and Caesar's too.[78]

But what happens at Niagara that transforms the innocent maiden into a wife? Surely passion is involved, but passion that has been shaped and enclosed within a ritual code,[79] thus aiding in preservation of the social order.

Perhaps passion exacts a certain compensation for this confinement. The virginal purity of the bride that Howell and others have emphasized may help her to serve as a symbolic offering.[80] The figure of the pure virgin also appears in the legend of the

Indian Maid of the Mist, a legend that first appeared at the same time as the practice of honeymooning at Niagara. According to the legend, which is a mid-Victorian white man's invention,[81] the fairest virgin of the tribe must be sent over the falls in a canoe to appease the Spirit of the Falls. In a late-nineteenth-century poem by William Trumbull, the Spirit lives beneath the "eternal sweep of the waters" which "throbs in rhythmic measure." The "children of the forest" hear the Spirit's demand:

> Deep were borne the Spirit's mutterings,
> > calling fierce for human blood;
> Ay, and sacrifice more cruel in that cry,
> > they understood:
> Gift of Nature's choicest treasure,
> > peerless budding womanhood![82]

In an 1882 version of the story, George Houghton, an editor and writer from New York City, described this virgin gift as a "vow." The tribe, he wrote,

> Chose from their fairest virgins the fairest and
> > purest among them,
> Hollowed a birchen canoe, and fashioned a seat for
> > the virgin,
> Clothed her in white, and set her adrift to whirl to
> > thy bosom,
> Saying: "Receive this our vow, Niagara, Father of
> > the Waters!"[83]

A final example, "Niagara's Rainbow" (1922)—a poem by New Hampshire surgeon Willard Parker—connects the legend to the biblical story of the Flood. When the "fairest blossom" of the tribe plunges over the cataract's brink, the "spirit's rainbow" appears signaling that a covenant has been established.[84] Marriage, too, is like a covenant, not only between a man and a woman, but also between humanity and nature. Perhaps the symbolic gift of the unstained virgin is meant to bribe the wild forces of nature to keep within their banks, to accept the confinement of the vows.

The Nature of Niagara

One of the few modernist works on Niagara Falls, Michael Butor's novel, *Niagara* (1965),[85] offers a final perspective on the theme of sex and marriage at Niagara. Along with several other French novelists of the late 1950s, Butor was trying to create a new kind of literature—the *nouveau roman*.[86] His example of that form is a subtle exploration of modern illusions about sex and romance. Butor calls it a "stereophonic novel," in which several "channels" are "playing" simultaneously. Each channel occupies a number of columns on the printed page. On one channel, throughout the novel, we "hear" Chateaubriand's description of the falls from his novel *Atala* or *The Love of Two Savages in the Wilderness* (1801).[87] The other channels are taken up with dialogue, mostly between couples, and the voice of an announcer who describes various events and scenes of Niagara's tourist season.

Everyone in this novel is thinking about sex. Some are anticipating it; some are remembering it; some, awakening from their wedding night, are thinking of their first taste of sex; and some, just married, still look forward to the experience. Several characters repeatedly examine "little naked porcelain women whose breasts come off to make salt and pepper shakers." We hear a young husband ask: "Why did you need lipstick to seduce me this morning?" His wife answers that she wanted her lips to be like "a crown of little flames that burn me." Butor continuously intertwines the chaos of nature and the chaos of passion. In one passage, for example, we hear the announcer saying: "Dark. Obsession, which prowls in the booming night," while Chateaubriand's words play on a second channel: "Over the chaos of the waves . . . Lake Erie . . . in the abyss . . . an enormous rock hollow underneath which hangs with all its pines . . ." (Butor's ellipses). And on a third channel, a young man speaks: "Stretch out on the bed, let me undress you, let me," and a woman answers: "No, help me to go back to my room."[88]

Most of the characters are beset with illusions about love; they expect it to be perfect. Their image of Niagara is one of the illusions. A woman tells her new husband: "I wanted absolutely to wait, my darling, until we got to this place . . . we couldn't stop in any old motel . . . I wanted it to be here."[89] In other words, she wanted to preserve her virginity until the perfect moment with the man who was destined to be her lifelong mate.

One of the strongest illusions in Butor's novel is that love will make you young. We see several old women who have come to Niagara with young lovers. One of these women explains why she is attracted to her young admirer: "I love you because you are nervous that way; you are a child, you could almost be my son." And another tells her young companion: "You are so inexperienced, a real little savage. Everything seems so wonderful to you." Old men are no different: "Leaning on the railing, a man no longer middle-aged," the announcer tells us, "gloats over a young girl." Finally, another old man observes: "All this water makes me give into this youth I never had." Butor also brings single people to Niagara. They have a particularly strong fascination with members of the opposite sex. One young man walking alone laments: "O all of you in your bedrooms entwined two by two; O all of you chained naked flesh to naked flesh, night unto night."[90]

Some characters become disillusioned. After an old couple fail in their attempt to make love, the woman despairs: "I think it's too late for us." Another accuses her husband: "I seemed to you very old, . . . very wrinkled, very faded, very decayed, admit it!" And one woman sees that even the young are not satisfied: "And if you looked at them carefully, you would soon see that they, too, need to be made young again."[91]

Butor's point is that, although these characters may become disillusioned with their partners or even with themselves, they never give up their illusions about romance. They imagine that involvement with the right member of the opposite sex will bring them salvation and make them whole. They expect too much. Yet once they have a romantic affair, it soon turns banal. Instead of reexamining their fascination, they look for another lover. As one character puts it: "Always another one, and each time it is the same disgust." And when a young man begins to wonder what he had seen in his elderly lover, she explains that "it wasn't so difficult to create an illusion for you."[92] The reason, of course, was that he supplied most of the illusion himself.

In the second chapter, we explored one reason for the presence of honeymooners at Niagara. The honeymoon—or the wedding journey, as it was usually called in the nineteenth century—is a kind of ritual rite of passage which, like pilgrimage, must take place outside of the structures of the ordinary world. Since many people had imagined Niagara Falls as a place beyond the boundaries of the ordinary world, it became an appropriate goal for both a pilgrimage and a wedding journey. Our present discussion suggests two more reasons for the prevalence of honeymooning at Niagara. The first begins with the recognition that a honeymoon is, among other things, a time for copulation. Many have seen Niagara as a symbol of the wild, natural side of human nature— often explicitly as a symbol of the sexual passions—which must be subdued to preserve the order and harmony of the human world. The institution of marriage is one attempt to preserve this order and harmony. A honeymoon at Niagara Falls allows the newly married couple to witness the power of nature, and by analogy, the power of passion. They therefore see the need to constrain their passions by adhering to the wedding vows.

A final reason for Niagara's appropriateness as a honeymoon site is suggested by Butor's novel. The appeal of romance, like Niagara's own appeal, depends upon imagination. The opposite sex is fascinating simply because it is opposite, because it is remote. One can imagine the romantic affair, like the first sight of Niagara Falls, as something entirely novel, having no connection with past or present experience. The romantic belief that there is one perfect mate who will make each person's life complete is crucial to the institution of marriage, especially in a society where the forces of tradition that once made marriage sacrosanct have eroded. But this romantic belief, like some travelers' image of Niagara Falls, is not likely to come true. "Every American bride is taken [to Niagara Falls]," Oscar Wilde wryly observed, "and the sight of the stupendous waterfall must be one of the earliest, if not the keenest, disappointments in American married life."[93]

five

THE FUTURE AT NIAGARA

*T*he sight of Niagara Falls reminded some nineteenth-century travelers of the flow of time. As the Connecticut visitor James Dixon commented in 1849, Niagara was "a power, concentrating itself . . . sweeping along . . . like the mighty stream of time, bearing the fate and destiny of nature and empires into the abyss below, the hades of all created things." The falls in this analogy represented a break in the "stream of time," a threshold no one could see beyond. The abyss beneath the falls, Dixon continued, was "a frightful gulf, scooped out as if to embrace the descending flood, and conduct it to some new destiny:—as the present receives the past in its passage onward, and impels it by a new impulse, together with all it bears on its tide, to the mysterious future."[1]

Beyond the break in the stream of time lay the indeterminate world of the future. Although this world was invisible to human eyes, many of Niagara's visitors were fascinated by it. Some regarded this as a dangerous fascination. Consider, for example, this anonymous poetic description of Niagara from 1861:

The Future of Niagara

In vain—the foam turns marble as it rolls, And, like the Future from the Present hidden, It bears this lesson to our struggling souls—Seek not the knowledge to thy state forbidden.[2]

Although this image of the future as remote and mysterious appeared early in the nineteenth century, it was not until the beginning of hydroelectric power development in the 1890s that the idea of the future really became bound up with Niagara Falls. People began to speculate about what lay beyond the break in time that Niagara's brink represented, and they began to imagine various futures in which Niagara was to play a central role. At first, these visions of the future were almost uniformly optimistic. Usually proposed by scientists, entrepreneurs, and engineers, they took the form of massive utopian development schemes. After the turn of the century, some negative visions of the future began to appear at Niagara, usually finding expression in poems and novels. Yet, the optimistic view clearly dominated, particularly among those people who played major roles in shaping Niagara's landscape.

It is not altogether surprising that the future captured people's imaginations at Niagara Falls. Like an unknown world beyond the ocean or beyond death's door, the future is a remote realm where things that are clearly impossible in the here and now might be considered feasible. The multitude of visions of the future that began to emerge near the end of the nineteenth century were thus part of the long tradition of imagining Niagara as remote. All the perceptions of Niagara—as a distant goal, as a reminder of death, as an embodiment of Nature, and as a focus of the future—are, in a sense, facets of a single perception. They express a single fascination with the world beyond the limits of ordinary knowledge and experience.

This chapter will examine the visions of the future that appear in the literature of Niagara Falls. But the purpose will be more than literary, for we will also explore the connection between the future these writers imagined for Niagara and the future that actually emerged, particularly with regard to Niagara's economic and industrial development.

Contemporary visitors are often surprised at the extent to

which Niagara's landscape is given over to industry. Even the river itself has been appropriated: in the course of a year, a great deal more water finds its way into turbines than reaches the brink of the falls. Since the 1890s, Niagara has been vigorously developed. The result, especially on the American side, is a very gritty landscape—in some areas, even a poisonous one. This industrial development is partly the product of Niagara's location and the timing of particular technological innovations. But the fact that Niagara could be so idealized as a natural object and yet so thoroughly exploited for human purposes presents itself to many as a grim paradox. My contention here is that industrial development and idealization are intimately connected. Visions of the future began as an extension of Niagara's idealization. Many of these visions led to action—action that eventually transformed the landscape of Niagara Falls, although perhaps not in ways that had been foreseen. The fall's industrial development depended upon a host of factors that could be examined through traditional economic and locational analysis, but this development was also a matter of imagination. It was in part because so many had their eyes on an imagined future, that Niagara realized the future it did.

Before examining specific visions of the future from Niagara's literature, let us consider briefly the broader context from which they emerged. Earlier perceptions of Niagara provided a fertile soil for the growth of these images of the future, but there were other reasons why they appeared at the end of the nineteenth century.

The last quarter of the nineteenth century was a time of great anticipation throughout the industrialized world, one indication of which was the blossoming of a futuristic literature. The enormous success of Jules Verne's *Five Weeks in a Balloon* in 1863 touched off a steady stream of tales of the future. By the 1890s, the stream had swelled to a flood. Technical forecasts and serious utopian proposals also formed part of this literature, which continued to grow until World War I.[3] The writings on the future of Niagara were part of this burgeoning literature.

The future, in this literature, was presented as a vast realm of possibility, but such an image would have been entirely alien to the medieval imagination. The apocalyptic traditions of the Middle Ages promised an intrusion of eternity into time, a cataclysmic rupture of the present order, but this was not a future about which one could speculate; it was part of a divine plan.[4] An increasing ability to control nature first gave Europeans an inkling that the future might be totally unlike the past or present. Charles Beard, in his introduction to J. B. Bury's classic book, *The Idea of Progress,* put it this way: "It was not until commerce, invention and natural science emancipated humanity from the thralldom to the cycle and to the Christian epic that it became possible to think of an immense future for mortal mankind."[5] Apart from Christian dogma, another obstacle to a new conception of the future was the notion that the ancient world had been the zenith of civilization. The scientific discoveries of the sixteenth and seventeenth centuries—the work of Harvey, Kepler, and Galileo—helped to diminish the stature of the classical world. And, as Clarence Glacken has pointed out, geographical discoveries also played an important role: how could the ancients be superior when they had not even known of the New World?[6]

Francis Bacon was among the first to examine the implications of these advances. He concluded in the early seventeenth century that "the empire of man over things is founded on the arts and sciences alone."[7] Bacon's ideal state, *The New Atlantis* (1620), was based on the systematic domination and exploitation of nature; its citizens sought "the knowledge of causes and secret motions of things, and the enlarging of the bounds of the human empire, to the effecting of all things possible."[8] Bacon's writings reflected the fact that the world had changed and was still changing, yet his conception of the future, like his New Atlantis, was static. Bernard de Fontenelle was the first to extend the idea of progress into the future. Writing at the end of the seventeenth century, Fontenelle argued that progress was in the nature of things; it was necessary and certain.[9]

The eighteenth century saw further discoveries and technological improvements; canals were constructed in England and on the continent; the process of industrialization was initiated. These changes attracted more adherents to the idea of progress.

In 1770, Sabastien Mercier produced the first utopian tale of the future, *The Year 2440;* there were no slaves or wars in his twenty-fifth-century world, but neither were there any great scientific nor technological improvements. But by the end of the eighteenth century, men like Benjamin Franklin and the Marquis de Condorcet were predicting everything from birth control to antigravity devices to accompany the moral perfection of the future world.[10]

The idea of progress was controversial as it developed in the eighteenth century, but by the opening of the London Exposition of 1851, it had come to dominate the image of the future in both Europe and America. Historian J. B. Bury argued that scientific and mechanical progress conditioned nearly everyone to expect "an indefinite increase of man's power over nature."[11] The idea that the world was progressing and would continue to progress morally also gained strength in the nineteenth century. New social welfare programs were instituted and there was a general feeling that superstition was being eliminated. The march of Western civilization across the globe was bringing these advances to all peoples.

In the last quarter of the nineteenth century, the world of the future captured the popular imagination as had the world beyond the oceans in an earlier era. The most detailed and original ideas about the future can be found in accounts of utopias rather than in adventure stories or technical forecasts. As a subgenre, the progressive utopian works that predicted world peace and vast technological advances were certainly the most numerous and popular. Perhaps the most influential of these was Edward Bellamy's *Looking Backward, 2000–1887* (1888).[12] The narrator of this story describes America in the year 2000; there are electric lights, radios, and a pervasive spirit of cooperation. Within three years of its publication, *Looking Backward* had inspired Bellamy Clubs throughout the United States and in many European countries, all organized to bring about the future that the book described.[13] Between 1888 and 1900, an unprecedented outpouring of futuristic utopian works followed, particularly in the United States. Kenneth Roemer, who has recently examined these works, suggests that what is most surprising about them, from a late-twentieth-century perspective, is "the faith in man's ability to obtain the all—the literal belief in utopia as an attainable goal."[14]

Roemer also discovered that many people of this era, particularly in the United States, expected a kind of "final transition," a complete rupture from the past.[15] The conquest of nature seemed nearly complete: industrial civilization had changed the material face of the world, spreading itself over vast new continents. Now the ends of continents were being reached; the frontier was disappearing. The New World turned out to be a finite one, but the impending limits to growth appeared to many as a threshold, beyond which they imagined a "final transition," an endless vista of expansion. Late-nineteenth-century utopians believed that material progress had caused much human misery and created great confusion, but they interpreted the confusion as an opportunity, believing firmly that material progress would ultimately provide the basis for an ideal social order.

The hydroelectric development of Niagara in the late 1890s seemed to be a sort of capstone on humanity's victory over nature. The process of increasing human control over nature was finally turned on this last stronghold of natural power. For some observers, the development of Niagara represented the beginning of a new, totally human order.

Ironically, these forward-looking people clung to a view of nature that had been popular throughout the nineteenth century, particularly at Niagara—the idea that nature was unfathomable and inexhaustible. We might consider this notion a corollary of the idea of progress, for only if nature is limitless can we expect perpetual progress in our conquest of it. This interpretation leaves no room for a transition, however. Thus, those who expected a qualitative change to accompany the final conquest of nature also accepted that nature was limitless, but they believed that humanity could appropriate nature's power for itself. The immense potential of nature was to be transformed into human potential.

Nearly everyone who wrote about the future in the nineteenth century believed in the idea of progress. "The spectacular results of the advance of science and mechanical technique," wrote J. B. Bury, "brought home to the mind of the average man the conception of an indefinite increase in man's power over nature as his brain penetrated her secrets."[16] People also expected great moral and social progress to arise concurrently. As early as 1851, for instance, the Great Exposition at London had aroused a widespread feeling of impending social transformation. Queen Victoria's husband, the Prince Consort, summed up this sense of expectation when he commented: "We are living at a period of most wonderful transition, which tends rapidly to accomplish that great end to which all history points—the realization of the unity of mankind."[17]

The idea that the future would be materially as well as morally superior to the present certainly dominated the literature on the future at Niagara Falls. Yet in this literature, as well as in the wider literature of the future, there arose some questions about the world that human control would create. The questioners were clearly in the minority, especially in the beginning, but they raised issues that are still with us.

The section that follows focuses on visions of a fabulous future at Niagara Falls from the pre-World War I era. The next section examines pessimistic images of the future from the same period. A final section examines ideas of the future at Niagara from the post–World War I period.

Nikola Tesla, the Yugoslavian-born inventor of alternating current, predicted in the mid-1890s that electricity generated at Niagara would one day power the streetcars of London and the streetlights of Paris. "Humanity will be like an ant heap stirred up with a stick," the passionate Tesla exclaimed. "See the excitement coming!"[18] Tesla, who himself designed the system which George Westinghouse adopted for the first transmission of electrical power from Niagara Falls in 1896,[19] was not alone in his excitement about the harnessing of Niagara. Most observers believed that stirring up the ant heap would ultimately bring wonderful results. Benjamin Copeland's poem, "Niagara" (1904), typified this spirit of unabashed optimism:

Our dreams exceeding by the bounteous sway;
With power unrivaled thy proud flood shall speed
The New World's progress toward Time's perfect day.[20]

Because of the previous sense of expectation in the late nineteenth century, the development of Niagara led people to imagine an expansive future. Yet some people had been excited much earlier about the prospects of tapping the cataract's power, at least for the immediate vicinity of Niagara Falls.

For example, in 1799 the Duke of Liancourt concluded after visiting Niagara that its capacity for industrial development, like the power of its waters, was "almost boundless."[21] This perception was echoed repeatedly throughout the nineteenth century.[22] The settlers who, in 1805, founded the village on the American side of the falls agreed with Liancourt, and named the place after the greatest industrial center they knew, Manchester. One early reason for optimism was the authorization by the New York State legislature in 1798 of a plan to build a canal around the falls within ten years.[23] Although surveys were completed in 1808 and again in 1826, the plan lapsed because of financial problems; the state had turned its attention to the Erie Canal.[24] In 1853, Niagara's representative to the state legislature, George W. Holley, pushed through a funding bill for a much more ambitious project. In addition to the ship canal, Holley planned to supply "inexhaustible" water power for a large manufacturing center at Lewiston—a "second Manchester"—which was to be known as a "city of fountains."[25] Political tensions between the northern and southern states leading to the Civil War prevented this plan from being realized.

In the late nineteenth century, several water power plants finally got beyond the planning stage. These projects at once embodied and stimulated the image of Niagara as the place where the future was about to happen. Actual developments at Niagara stirred many to imagine vast future developments. But all of these visions—those that materialized as well as the ones that remained dreams—were inspired by an image of Niagara as an inexhaustible natural force, something to be imagined rather than measured.

The first large industrial development at Niagara Falls had its beginnings in 1847 when Judge Augustus Porter, who owned a great deal of land near the cataract's brink, published a circular—

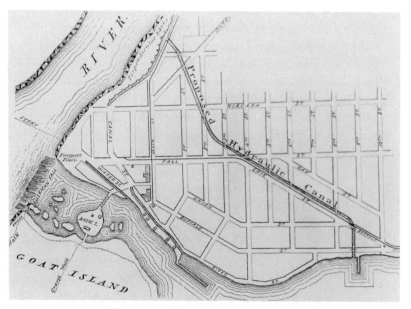

5. Map of Niagara Falls, New York, showing proposed
hydraulic canal, 1846, by P. Emslie. From Edward Dean
Adams, *Niagara Power* (Niagara Falls, N.Y.: Niagara Falls
Power Company, 1927), p. 46.

"To Capitalists and Manufacturers"—offering a right-of-way
suitable for a power canal nearly a mile in length.[26] Accompany-
ing the circular was a map showing the route of the proposed
canal (figure 5). The map, drawn by P. Emslie in 1846, clearly
depicts the paucity of industry at Niagara at this time. All of the
mills were located either in the islands of the upper rapids or
along two small raceways that emptied back into the river above
the crest of the falls. Among the structures were several small
textile mills and machine shops, a flour mill, a paper mill, and a
sawmill.[27] Porter had issued a similar invitation to investors in
1825, in which he had claimed: "Practically speaking, the extent
to which water-power may be applied is without limit. A thousand mills might be erected with the same ease [as one]."[28]

A group of financiers headed by former New York City mayor
Caleb S. Woodhull signed a contract to build a hydraulic canal at

Niagara in 1852. The following year they began excavation with the idea that Niagara Falls would soon become "one of the great workshops of the world, sending forth daily the wonderful creations of human industry and skill."[29] Slow progress and lack of funds forced the hydraulic canal project through several owners, and it was not until 1875 that the first mill began operation. By 1882, there were seven flour and paper mills using almost 3,000 horsepower. Utilization continued to increase until the mid-1890s. The canal was widened in 1895, and the following year a large hydroelectric plant began to transmit direct-current electrical power for a nascent aluminum industry, a railway, and the streetlights of Niagara Falls, New York.[30] When finally completed in 1901, the plant delivered 31,250 h.p. Beginning in 1904, the canal was enlarged again to enable a new power plant to produce 130,000 h.p., although this level of generation was not realized until the installation was completed in 1914.[31]

This hydraulic canal allowed the first large-scale utilization of Niagara's power, but it was soon dwarfed by a new project that diverted water in an entirely new way. In 1886, Thomas Evershed, a division engineer of the Erie Canal, outlined a novel plan for power utilization at the falls. More than any proposal before or since, Evershed's scheme fired the imaginations of capitalists, engineers, and utopian planners. His idea was to construct a deep tunnel beginning at the level of the lower river near the foot of the American Falls, and extending two and one-half miles beneath the village of Niagara Falls to a point along the upper river where water could be diverted through a series of vertical shafts into the tunnel (figure 6 and figure 7).[32] Evershed calculated that the tunnel could accommodate 238 mills with a total of 119,000 h.p.[33] A group of local promoters immediately seized on the plan and acquired the necessary land as well as a charter from the state of New York. But, unable to raise enough capital for such an ambitious scheme, they sold their holdings in 1889 to a group of New York capitalists headed by banker Edward Dean Adams. This group formed the Niagara Falls Power Company.

From the outset, Adams and his associates approached the project from an entirely new perspective. Past methods and experience, they felt, could shed little light on an engineering

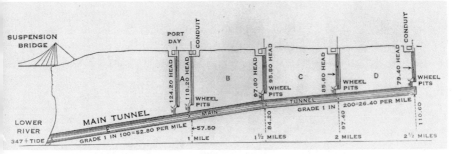

6. Power Tunnel, cross-sectional view. From Edward Dean
Adams, *Niagara Power* (Niagara Falls, N.Y.: Niagara Falls
Power Company, 1927), p. 114.

enterprise this massive. They began by consulting a series of
experts, including Thomas Edison, about the best way to develop
water power at Niagara. The power company permanently retained many of these distinguished scientists and engineers as an
advisory board. Preliminary consultations resulted in three rec-
ommendations: that power should be generated at a central
station rather than at hundreds of mills; second, that it should be
generated as electrical as opposed to mechanical power; and
third, that a method of transmitting the power to Buffalo should
be sought. The need to gain a relatively fast return on invest-
ments made this last recommendation necessary. The population
of Niagara Falls in 1890 was only 5,000, while Buffalo's was over
250,000. The power company hoped eventually to establish a
large manufacturing center at Niagara Falls, but Buffalo offered
an immediate market. The leaders of the power company, also
decided to begin construction of the tunnel while proceeding to
research the questions of power generation and transmission.[34]

In 1890, as the digging commenced, Adams sailed to investi-
gate the latest electrical developments in Europe. He formed a
kind of think tank, headquartered in London, called the "International Niagara Commission," the purpose of which was to find
the best system for hydroelectric development at Niagara Falls.
It included representatives from four nations and was headed
by the distinguished British scientist Lord Kelvin (Sir William

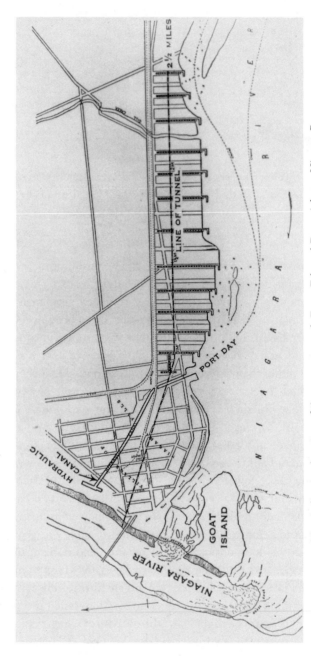

7. Map indicating location of the power tunnel. From Edward Dean Adams, *Niagara Power* (Niagara Falls, N.Y.: Niagara Falls Power Company, 1927), p. 114.

Thomson). The power company issued an invitation to developers and inventors, offering a $100,000 prize for the winning entry. In 1891, the commission awarded eight prizes, although it found no proposal acceptable in its entirety.[35]

The electrical generators that were finally adopted sat atop vertical pits and were turned by long shafts connected to turbines resting at the bottom. Power generation was only a minor problem compared with the difficulties posed by long-distance transmission. Against the advice of both Edison and Kelvin, the company selected alternating-current over direct-current transmission. George Westinghouse, who had adopted Nikola Tesla's transmission system, received a contract in 1895 to generate alternating current at Niagara Falls; power generation began later that year. By 1896, power lines to Buffalo were complete and long-distance transmission commenced. The power was first used for lighting Buffalo's streets.[36]

The leaders of the Niagara Falls Power Company had more in mind than power generation. They secured vast tracts of land, which soon became the home of a large electrochemical complex.[37] In addition, they built an electric railway and a new residential town. The town was named Echota, the Cherokee word for "Town of Refuge." Echota featured a New York Central passenger station and workers' houses designed by architect Stanford White, who also created a color scheme for painting all the houses in the town.

By 1903, power installations on the American side of the falls had reached a total capacity of 101,500 h.p. The Canadian capacity was a mere 2,000 h.p., but during this same year, three large hydroelectric power houses were under construction in Canada.[38] The Canadian Niagara Power Company, which had broken ground in 1901, was a subsidiary of the Niagara Falls Power Company. Like its American counterpart, it installed a tunnel system with generators placed at the tops of wheel pits. When the Canadian Niagara plant began operating in 1904, all of its power was transmitted back across the river for American use.[39]

The Ontario Power Company began construction of a second Canadian power plant in 1902. This company adopted the model of the hydraulic power company on the American side, with one difference. Instead of a canal, an intake tunnel ran near the surface to a point adjacent to the Horseshoe Falls, where the water was then forced down penstocks turning generators at the foot of the gorge. When the Ontario Power Company began electrical generation in 1905, most of the power went back across the river—some to points as distant as Syracuse.

A third company, the Electrical Development Company (later the Toronto Power Company), began building a power plant in 1903 and delivered its first power in 1906. Following the examples of the Niagara Falls Power Company and its Canadian subsidiary, this new plant used vertical shafts, capped with generators, connected to a deep tunnel. Constructing the discharge tunnel, which opened right behind the Horseshoe Falls, proved a very tricky problem and nearly scuttled the project.[40]

By 1908, total power generation on the Canadian side had surpassed that of the American side.[41] Yet it is indicative of the nature of Canadian power development, primarily for export, that the Village of Niagara Falls, Ontario, continued to generate its own electricity by steam until 1912.

As noted previously, the preservation movement of the 1870s and early 1880s led to the creation of the Niagara Reservation in New York (1885) and Queen Victoria Park in Ontario (1887). The preservationists succeeded in removing the water-powered mills from the immediate brink of the falls and from the islands of the rapids. These mills had been in place before 1875 when the hydraulic canal was first utilized. The loss of these mills was only a minor blow to local industry, for, by 1885, the canal provided ample opportunity for expansion. Yet the preservationists continued to view industry as an adversary. From the beginning they opposed the Evershed scheme. The prospect of 238 factories worried them. They were concerned about visual blight, but they were more concerned about the flow of the river itself. To shrink Niagara's volume, they felt, was to destroy its majesty, its power as a spectacle. The preservationists were even more deeply worried when the president of the International Niagara Commission, Lord Kelvin, made the following statement:

The Future of Niagara

I look forward to the time when the whole water from Lake Erie will find its way to the lower level of Lake Ontario through machinery, doing more good for the world than even the great benefit which we now possess in the contemplation of the splendid scene which we have before us in the waterfall of Niagara. I wish I could live to see this grand development. I do not hope that our children's children will ever see the Niagara cataract.[42]

The chasm separating the two sides can be seen by comparing Kelvin's view to that of Frederick Law Olmsted, a leading preservationist. Olmsted has been hired by New York State to create a general plan for the Niagara Reservation. He wrote:

Not park, nor pleasure ground, but "Reservation" is the name affixed by the Legislature to the property now happily recovered to the people. It is a spot reserved, and sacred to what divine power has already placed there, rather than a proper field for the display of human ingenuity or art.[43]

Just after the turn of the century, when large-scale diversion for power generation had become a reality, a new preservation movement began to gather force. "Saved from the hands of the catch-penny sharper," as one writer put it, Niagara had now fallen "into the hands of the catch-million capitalist."[44] Preservationists alleged that the power situation at Niagara had come under the grip of "the Vanderbilt-Astor-Morgan group."[45] "Niagara Falls are doomed," wrote Alton D. Adams in a 1905 article in *Cassier*'s. "Children already born may yet walk dry-shod from the mainland of the New York State Reservation to Goat Island, across the present bed of the Niagara River."[46] The preservationists agreed that only government action could prevent Niagara's demise, and they lobbied for an international treaty to limit diversion.

This second preservation movement inspired two government actions. The first was a report submitted to Congress in 1909 by the war department recommending that a national park be established at Niagara Falls.[47] That recommendation never came to a vote. The second action began with a report to Congress on the preservation of Niagara Falls, submitted by President Roosevelt in 1906.[48] With some modifications, his proposal was adopted later that year when Congress passed the Burton Act. Under the provisions of this law, water diversions on the New York side of Niagara Falls could not exceed 15,600 cubic feet per second. This amounted to a freeze on power development, although it allowed diversion for projects under construction in 1906. The United States eventually signed a treaty with Great Britain in 1909, limiting total American diversion to 20,000 c.f.s.; the Canadians were allowed 36,000 c.f.s.[49]

Even after the international treaty, American power companies were subject to the more stringent restrictions of the Burton Act. But, during World War I, President Wilson ordered that all power capable of being produced at Niagara be directed to the war industries.[50] After the war ended, the Federal Water Power Act of 1920 increased diversion rights to the limits of the international treaty, and allowed the power companies to calculate their daily maximum as a yearly average. This allowed them to exceed 20,000 c.f.s. by as much as 5,000 c.f.s. on a given day. The Federal Water Power Act remained in effect until World War II.

The impact of diversion limits and the pressures of wartime growth in power demand forced both the American and Canadian power companies to strive for efficiency. Because some of the companies with diversion rights were very inefficient producers, amalgamation followed by a gradual transference of water to the most efficient plants seemed the only solution. The American companies joined together in 1918 to form the Niagara Falls Power Company. By 1925 this new company was producing twice as much horsepower from the same amount of water.[51] One by one, the Canadian power companies were bought out by the publicly owned Hydro-Electric Power Commission of Ontario. By 1925, the commission controlled seven-eighths of Canadian power generation at Niagara.[52]

We have reviewed water power developments at Niagara through the First World War in some detail, in part, to set the stage for a presentation of more visionary proposals from the same period that were never implemented. Yet the successful proposals were also imaginative. Like the more explicitly utopian schemes, they were based on a belief that the future would be both more fantastic and more humane than the present as a result of humanity's increasing ability to subdue nature and to transform its energy to human purposes.

The possibility of harnessing Niagara Falls stirred the imaginations of those entrepreneurs and engineers actually involved in the power projects. There was a sense of newness about the whole idea of capturing Niagara's power. Experts had to be consulted at every turn; the past had become insignificant. Humanity was to be, in Nikola Tesla's phrase, "like an ant heap stirred up with a stick." Even workers were to have new lives in the model town of Echota.

The way these people thought of the falls itself certainly contributed to their excitement over its development. Throughout the eighteenth and nineteenth centuries, people had viewed Niagara as much with their imaginations as with their eyes. From far away or from its very brink, Niagara was a symbol of something unlimited that lay beyond their grasp: death, nature, or indeed the future. As late as 1894, scientists were claiming that the potential power of Niagara Falls was equal to all the steam-generated power in the world.[53] To tap the virtually unlimited was itself an act of imagination. In an address before the Buffalo Society of Natural Sciences in 1903, prominent civil engineer A. Howell Van Cleve described Evershed's scheme as "an aqueduct such as was never before built in the history of man—a conception such as could only come to a man with an imagination, an imagination touched by the inspiration of the great cataract within whose sound he had toiled so long."[54] In a sense, Van Cleve was right: because people saw the falls as a thing of overwhelming majesty, the possibility of capturing that majesty lifted even scientists and engineers from their usual prosaic view of things. By the turn of the century, the power houses had become known as the "new Niagara."[55] Clearly, many who were directly involved with the creation of the "new Niagara" hoped it would retain the magic of the old Niagara.

One of the most striking expressions of the way the people behind the power developments viewed the harnessing of Niagara was a mural that graced the walls of the Schoellkopf Station, courtesy of the Niagara Falls Power Company (figure 8).[56] Ed-

8. Willy Pogany, "The Birth of Power," a mural which
decorated the walls of the Schoellkopf Power Station. From
Edward Dean Adams, *Niagara Power* (Niagara Falls, N.Y.:
Niagara Falls Power Company, 1927), frontispiece.

ward Dean Adams, the president of the company, described the
mural in these words:

> This allegorical painting tells in vivid and powerful tone, but
> with eerie lightness, the romantic birth story of humanity's
> modern servant—electrical power.
> Torrents of energy tumble into the eddying pool of human
> waves from which emerge the two poles imparting the spark
> of life to the giant genie—POWER.[57]

A genie indeed! By harnessing Niagara, the leaders of the power company felt they had acquired a power that, like Aladdin's, was almost magical and with which they could transform the world. Clearly this dramatic gain in power signaled a break with the past; now the future was entirely in human hands. The genie was the "new Niagara"; he embodied all the power of the old but none of the darkness. The hydroelectric development of Niagara transmuted the chaotic power of the falling water into a controlled and focused force. By using the very power of nature, humanity was able to rise above it.

In 1851 George William Curtis had watched an intrepid little steamer carrying tourists to the foot of the falls and had commented: "For man is the magician, . . . he dips his hand into Niagara, and gathering a few drops from its waters, educes a force from Niagara itself, by which he confronts and defies it."[58] When electricity was first generated in 1879, it was supplied to neither households nor industries. Instead, the energy was used to operate arc lamps at Prospect Point, where, by means of reflectors, electric light was shone on the falls itself.[59] This complex gesture was either an act of homage or an act of defiance. If the latter, it had little more effect than spitting into the wind. The genie in the power house mural is clearly defiant, but he is no longer spitting into the wind; he has triumphed over the falls.

We cannot understand power developments at Niagara without taking into account perceptions of the falls and perceptions of the future. Developers believed that subduing and harnessing Niagara's seemingly unlimited power would allow humanity to create a marvelous future. Yet, as this vision of the future was implemented, it was tempered by reality. We can best understand the vision that helped to inspire Niagara's development by examining some of the futuristic plans that were never implemented. In these plans we can see the vision fully crystallized, precisely because they were not forced to conform to the exigencies of the actual.

Plans to make Niagara Falls a great industrial metropolis surfaced from time to time throughout the nineteenth century. I have already discussed George W. Holley's idea of using Niagara's "inexhaustible" water power to create "a city of fountains" at Lewiston. Another visionary proposed that the falls be harnessed to one colossal water wheel and that this wheel be attached to a drive shaft 280 miles long! Local industries from Niagara Falls to Albany could then connect their own machinery to the shaft with belts.[60]

In the 1880s, development proposals began to appear with much greater regularity. One called for a huge port city at Lewiston with four miles of docks and complete exploitation of Niagara's power potential. Another scheme required the excavation of caves behind Niagara Falls; in this way, it was hoped, electrical generators could operate unseen behind the falling water, thus utilizing nearly all of Niagara's power without affecting its appearance. Developers collected over $20 million in investments, but—despite the support of many local landowners—this project never reached the construction stage.[61]

Many development proposals of the 1880s greatly overestimated both the fall's power and the abilities of engineers. A clear example of these tendencies was a project initiated by the City of Buffalo in 1882, to dig a fifteen-mile tunnel from Buffalo that would end behind the falls. The tunnel was to have two purposes: to carry away the city's sewage and to provide a tailrace for an enormous industrial development on Grand Island (the largest island in the Niagara River). The backers of the enterprise believed that thousands of mills and factories would be built, and that these, in turn, would transform Buffalo into a city of 5 million.[62]

Three proposals from the 1890s illustrate how Niagara's future became a showcase of both material and moral progress.[63]

In 1893 a flamboyant entrepreneur named William T. Love released an investment prospectus under the title "The Model City—Niagara Power Doubled."[64] Love claimed to have a development fund of over $25 million to support his project, and he proclaimed: "Nothing approaching it in magnitude, perfection or power has ever before been attempted."[65]

This Model City plan did indeed dwarf all previous development schemes, at least in the amount of urban acreage it proposed

The Future of Niagara

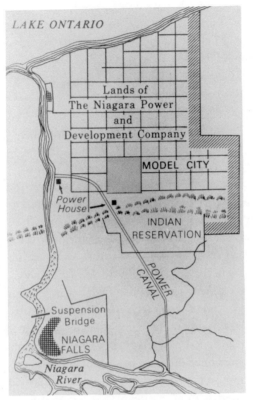

9. Map of Model City. Adapted by Eliza McClennen from the
original by William T. Love in the *Model City Bulletin,*
August 10, 1895, p. 12.

to develop. Love actually purchased a huge tract of land extending from the Niagara Escarpment to Lake Ontario—comprising
almost ninety square miles (figure 9). His plan was to dig a
navigable power channel from the upper Niagara River to this
site, thus utilizing the drop of the upper and lower rapids as well
as the drop of the falls itself. To attract industries, he offered free
sites and free power.[66] The city itself was to be very carefully
planned, a "Model City" with room for a million inhabitants.

Love, a very skillful promoter, often gave public speeches
accompanied by brass bands, circulars, and a chorus offering new
words to "Yankee Doodle": "Everybody's come to town, / Those

left we all do pity, / For we'll have a jolly time / At Love's new Model City."[67] Love constantly appealed to his audience's image of Niagara. Model City was "destined to become one of the greatest manufacturing cities of the United States," he wrote in the Model City Bulletin in 1895, because its developers were backed by "the great water power of Niagara Falls."[68] Commenting on Love's sales technique, Edward Dean Adams, president of the rival Niagara Falls Power Company, perceptively observed that "the word Niagara" suggested "such related words as colossal, inexhaustible, opportunity, power, fortune."[69] For Love, Niagara offered "the unequalled location in all the world for a great manufacturing city."[70] He promised "unlimited waterpower" with the risk of loss entirely eliminated.[71]

Love also appealed to his audience's progressive image of the future. Human control over nature would bring marvelous changes, and in the very near future. Model City was to undergo "rapid development" such as no other city in the world has ever experienced. And its very name, Model City, indicated that it was to be more than an embodiment of material progress. As Love stated in his original prospectus, it was to be a planned community, "designed to be the most perfect city in existence."[72] Considering the time, effort, and capital he invested, it is likely that Love himself shared both an image of Niagara and an image of the future with his audience.

The success of Love's pitch was remarkable. Somehow he persuaded the leaders of New York State to allow him the privilege of addressing a joint session of the legislature in 1893. After listening to his proposal, they granted him the right to condemn and appropriate whatever property was necessary and to divert as much water as he wanted.[73]

Construction commenced immediately at both ends of the canal. A factory, several homes, and about one mile of the canal were completed when the depression of the mid-1890s forced investors to withdraw their money. Love's company became bankrupt.[74] Ironically, Model City survives today as a tiny hamlet.

Perhaps the most elaborate of all visions of Niagara's future came from the inventive mind of the famous razor blade magnate,

The Future of Niagara

King Camp Gillette, who presented his plan in his 1894 book, *The Human Drift*.[75] Observing the growing concentration both of capital and of industrial production, Gillette concluded that eventually there could be only one corporation and one city in North America—perhaps even in the world. The site of this city, which he called Metropolis, would be Niagara Falls because that location offered a power source that Gillette considered almost infinite. He believed that the time was ripe for a great social change as well. If people as a whole could gain control of the great "World Corporation" that was rationalizing production and distribution, why could they not also provide material equality under conditions of great wealth? If Americans would only use their intelligence to transform the chaos of nature and the chaos of the competitive social and economic system, thought Gillette, they could create a perfect future world, a socialistic paradise. The great future city at Niagara, which Gillette estimated would eventually contain 60 million people, was to be the embodiment of this perfection, morally as well as materially.

Gillette was a man of contradictions. He eventually acquired enormous wealth through the competitive system he loathed. Yet it is worth noting that he published *The Human Drift* eight years before his revolutionary razor made him a financial success. Moreover, Kenneth Roemer has discovered an intriguing connection between Gillette's utopian scheme and his business scheme: each appeared to Gillette in a sudden flash of insight within a year of each other.[76]

As he neared the age of forty, Gillette had become increasingly obsessed with achieving a breakthrough of some kind, a big idea. The first insight came as he was watching traffic from a hotel window in Scranton, Pennsylvania. He fell into a reverie, tracing the products carried by trucks to their sources. In his words:

> Then came the thought that is destined to change man's conception of industry—THE THOUGHT—Industry as a whole is one vast operative mechanism. . . . The whole machine constitutes a system and to improve this machine means that we must change the system or displace it entirely with a better one. WORLD CORPORATION WOULD DISPLACE THE PRESENT SYSTEM AND ESTABLISH A BETTER ONE.[77]

The Future of Niagara

In the summer following the completion of *The Human Drift*, Gillette received his second insight. He had become obsessed with the idea of inventing something that would be needed by everyone, and that would have to be purchased over and over. One morning as he was about to shave, he found his razor dull:

> . . . it was beyond the point of successful stropping and it needed honing, for which it must be taken to a barber or to a cutler. As I stood there with the razor in my hand, my eyes rested on it lightly as a bird settling down on its nest—the Gillette razor was born. I saw it in a moment, and in that same moment many unvoiced questions were asked and answered more with the rapidity of a dream than by the slow process of reasoning. . . .[78]

Not only are these two visions similar in form, but, in one sense at least, in content as well. Roemer points out that the idea of a throwaway consumer item that is needed over and over again "is rooted in the 19th-century belief in the inexhaustible resources of Nature's Nation."[79] This belief also underlies Gillette's plan for Metropolis: here it is Niagara that is inexhaustible, as the power of the falls supports an entire continent.

Gillette's Metropolis merits more extensive analysis than the other proposals for two reasons. First, Gillette's plan was more elaborately worked out than any of the others; three volumes and several articles were devoted to its description.[80] The other reason is that Gillette took many notions that were common to all other proposals and carried them to their extreme, if logical, conclusions. His writings thus illustrate the implications of more widely held ideas and perceptions.

Like many of his contemporaries, Gillette felt that he was living in an unprecedented era of change. On the title page of *The Human Drift*, an epigram proclaims: "The very air we breathe is pregnant with life that foretells the birth of a wonderful change." And the book's first sentence reads: "We are rapidly nearing the most critical period in the history of this country." Gillette viewed the possibilities of change optimistically. He wanted to "step aside from the well-beaten track of ages" and create a movement that, if successful, "would mean a more radical change than is possible for the individual to conceive, and would separate the civilization of the near future from the present and past, by a gulf as wide as that which separates the two extremes of good and evil." The change would be a swift one, like "an earthquake that destroys cities and towns in a single night." On the last page of *The Human Drift*, Gillette issued a cry for revolution; he conjured the image of a perfect civilization lying just beyond a vortex in time:

> Come one, come all, and join the ranks of an overwhelming United People's Party. Let us start the ball rolling with such a boom and enthusiasm that it will draw the wealth and sinew of the nation into its vortex,—the great future city "Metropolis." . . . Forward! is the cry. "Let the dead past bury its dead," and let a new era of civilization and progress shed its light of hope on the future of mankind.[81]

The key to attaining the perfect future world was the application of human intelligence to all matters, whether material or moral. The birth of the World Corporation, he prophesied, would

> determine the great dividing line between the reign of brute and the reign of soul. It is the triumph of mind over matter and the birth of divinity in man. . . . Life will be worth living. Heaven will be on earth, . . . It is not a vision of the future, it is a vision of now. It is at our very door, and the door is open. The dawn of a new era streams across the threshold and lights the pathway to the future.[82]

The choice was between disaster and reason, and Gillette believed that there was some warrant for thinking that reason would win.

The "White City" at the 1893 Chicago World's Fair had demonstrated to Gillette's satisfaction that the technological possibilities of the future were vast and that, given a noble enterprise, people from all parts of the globe could cooperate. "The great exposition at Chicago," he wrote, "is an embryo illustration of the future great manufacturing centre of North America,—a perpetual World's Fair."[83] For Gillette, the exposition portended the victory of reason over instinct, mind over matter, intelligence over chaos. The front cover of *The Human Drift* bears this epigram: "The world is a diamond in the rough, and intellect, the only progressive entity, must cut the facets to discover its beauty and power."

But if intelligence was to be lifted so high, what was to become of that other nineteenth-century ideal, nature? Gillette answered that "the whole aspect of nature must assume new meanings and ends."[84] Now nature must be transformed by human artifice. "United Intelligence" must rise above nature and make the world its own, for mind is "infinite and eternal."[85] Yet, ironically, Gillette failed to escape from the nineteenth-century view of nature as an inexhaustible kingdom. For Gillette, nature—and Niagara itself—remained a diamond, albeit an uncut one. "Here is a power," he wrote, "which, if brought under control, is capable of keeping in continuous operation every manufacturing industry for centuries to come, and, in addition, supply all the lighting facilities, run all the elevators, and furnish the power necessary for the transportation system of the great central city."[86] Gillette, like Love, hoped that the falls would help sell his project. And, like his predecessor, he knew that the very word "Niagara" summoned up the image of a power impossible to overestimate. Hence, he included a photograph of the falls as the frontispiece in *The Human Drift.*

Gillette envisioned Metropolis as a city of such intelligence and artifice that it "would make London, Paris, Berlin, Vienna, and New York look like the work of ignorant savages in comparison."[87] Metropolis was to be the ultimate embodiment of intellect. It would replace chaos with order in two ways. First, it would replace the chaotic system of production and distribution with a perfectly logical and orderly one. Second, it would replace the chaotic natural landscape of Niagara Falls with a rational urban pattern.

The idea of Metropolis was itself the key to economic order and efficiency. "Under a perfect economical system of production and distribution," Gillette argued, "there can be only one city on a continent, and possibly only one in the world." He would not grant that competition, either among corporations or cities, was "the motive power of material progress." Rather, Gillette contended, competition created chaos and hence retarded progress.

Even the revolutionary transition to the new system was to be rational. Capital would flow to the World Corporation, and people would abandon their towns and cities for Metropolis, because, like "progressive manufacturers," they would "not hesitate to abandon an old machine for one of more modern construction."[88] Metropolis was to be the focus of a perfectly efficient economic system. Centralization would afford ultimate economics of scale. In the industrial district of Metropolis, which was to be centered on the falls itself, each manufacturing industry was to have its plant.[89] There would be only one steel mill, one flour mill, and one shoe factory in the whole of North America. As far as possible, each industry would be automated. Moreover, nearly all of the workers and consumers would live at the same site. The efficiency of this system, Gillette concluded, would result in the creation of great excess wealth. This wealth, in turn, would provide the basis for social progress by opening opportunities for all.

Gillette believed that "the mind is naturally virtuous, honest, ambitious, and progressive"; it is only circumstances that prevent social harmony. With excess wealth, a society could create "conditions of material equality" in which the people "would be rational in all their desires," for "they would no longer have an incentive to accumulate." For Gillette, material equality was the key to eliminating the social and moral dilemmas of humankind, "for civilization, under these conditions of equal opportunity, would be as full of life as a boiling cauldron, and all its dirt and filth would gradually rise to the top and disappear." Gillette considered labor the source of all material value, yet under the present system labor was enslaved.[90] Material equality, he believed, was the only alternative to class war.

Gillette proposed other social changes for his utopia. Women were to have full equality in all matters, be they legal, political, or economic. Since automation would reduce the need for physical labor, all the citizens of Metropolis would have the right to choose their occupation freely. Salary would not be a consideration in such a choice because everyone's material wants would be freely provided. Gillette represented the world of work in his Metropolis as an "Educational and Industrial Pyramid"; every person, no matter what kind of work he or she performed, would have equal access to the top of the pyramid, an equal chance to help administer the World Corporation. Since Metropolis was to be the heart of a socially "perfect" civilization, it would be "the home of all."[91] Social harmony, in short, would follow as a by-product of economic and industrial orderliness.

The second way that Metropolis would replace chaos with order was more concrete. In Gillette's eyes, the rapids and the falls made Niagara's landscape particularly chaotic. He regarded this as a waste of power and he planned to put all of the falling water to work, thus eliminating Niagara Falls itself. He intended to transform this natural landscape further by imposing a rational urban pattern: the shape of Metropolis was to be a perfect rectangle. Gillette's map (figure 10) shows a rectangular city 45 miles by 135 miles; its area is almost 6,000 square miles. The smaller rectangle (indicated by dotted lines) represents the residential section of Metropolis. This would be the home of 60 million people—the entire population of the United States in 1890. Gillette predicted that the city would eventually swell to 90 million.[92]

Many late-nineteenth-century utopias featured futuristic cities with symmetrical shapes. By far the most favored shape was the circle, and indeed Gillette changed the shape of Metropolis to a circle in his second book.[93] Kenneth Roemer suggests that utopians chose the circle, the square, and the rectangle not only because these shapes were orderly and simple but also because they symbolized changelessness. It was the "paradox of late nineteenth-century American utopianism," Roemer writes, to desire "rapid, multiple innovations coupled with a longing for security and changelessness."[94] Gillette was obviously calling for tremendous changes, but he also expressed a desire for security and freedom from change in at least two ways. The first, as we have seen, was the "eternal" shape he gave to Metropolis; the other was his designation of "durability of structure" as a matter of "first importance" in the construction of the city.

Metropolis was to have "a perfect system of sewage" that was "practically indestructible," a "perfect" and "indestructible" system of water distribution, heat-distribution, transportation, and

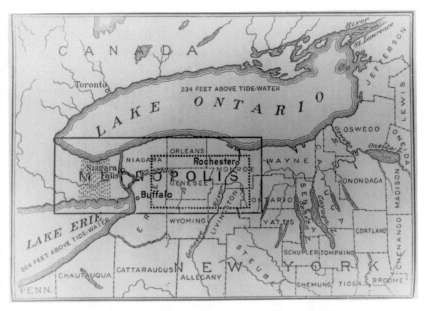

10. Map of Metropolis. From King Camp Gillette, *The Human Drift* (1894, Boston, New Era; reprint ed., Delmar, N.Y.: Scholar's Facsimiles & Reprints, 1976), p. 89.

electric telephone communication. The interior and exterior surfaces of every building were to be covered with porcelain because of its cleanliness and durability. Metropolis was to be a "city of porcelain." After describing in detail the construction of the typical apartment tower, Gillette proclaimed: "A building built as described would be practically indestructible, and I doubt if one thousand years would impair its usefulness or beauty." But it is in describing the World Corporation and the new civilization it would engender that Gillette carries this notion of durability to its extreme:

> Under these circumstances, the corporation has within it the elements of continuous life; for the death of any single or number of individuals would not disturb its progress. This same idea would also be true of a civilization that was combined as one intelligence. It would have the elements of continuous life, and nothing could disturb its continuous progress.[95]

The most dramatic expression of Gillette's intention of imposing order on the chaotic natural landscape of Niagara Falls was his plan to build a 100-foot platform covering the entire surface of Metropolis, even extending over the Niagara River. The platform was to be divided into three chambers. The lowest one, resting on the ground and extending upward twenty-five feet, would house sewers, water pipes, and electrical lines. The second chamber, again twenty-five feet high, would serve as a transportation corridor; Gillette proposed an extensive electric subway system. The top chamber, a full fifty feet in height, would be reserved for walking and recreation. Glass domes scattered over the upper surface of the platform would provide light for a perpetual garden. The surface itself would also be restricted to pedestrian and recreational traffic.[96]

On top of this featureless surface, as a geographer might expect, Gillette planned a hexagonal street pattern. In *The Human Drift,* he provided an illustration of a portion of the residential district (figure 11). Although the portion represented would house over 82,000 people, it amounts to only 13 percent of the entire residential district. Each building is circular and sits at the center of a hexagon. In addition to the apartment towers, there are educational buildings (marked A), amusement buildings (marked B), and provisions buildings (marked C). Each of these specific buildings serves the six apartment towers that surround it. Food, for instance, would be sent beneath the surface in tubes to central dining halls in each apartment tower. In Metropolis, no one would need to cook.

The apartment buildings are twenty-five stories. They are conceived as a series of towers joined at the back to form a circle (figure 12). New advances in steel frame construction made this vertical city plausible. In a later book, Gillette increased the height of these buildings to fifty stories.[97] Although he often claimed that his Metropolis required no great technological advances, Gillette was quick to adopt the latest trends and extend their range of application.

Allowing human intelligence full reign over the material world would produce a civilization that was not only durable, but also beautiful. Gillette did not doubt that art could surpass the

11. Residential plan of Metropolis. From King Camp Gillette,
The Human Drift (1894, Boston, New Era; reprint ed., Delmar,
N.Y.: Scholar's Facsimiles & Reprints, 1976), plate 1, p. 94.

beauty of nature. Metropolis was to be an aesthetic achievement, and he promoted it that way. At night, all of Metropolis "would be brilliant with a flood of electric light which would throw into soft relief the beauties of environment, and make of the whole, a fairyland." Metropolis was to be a full-grown version of Chicago's "White City" from the Columbian Exposition, "a never-ending city of beauty and cleanliness," "a perpetual World's Fair." The fifty-foot chamber just below the surface, where Metropolitans could stroll amid "urns of flowers" and "beautiful works of art and statuary," was to be "an endless gallery of loveliness."

12. Metropolis apartment building and surroundings. From
King Camp Gillette, *The Human Drift* (1894, Boston, New Era;
reprint ed., Delmar, N.Y.: Scholar's Facsimiles & Reprints,
1976), plate 5, p. 102.

"Here would be found a panorama of beauty that would throw
into shadow the fables of wonderful palaces and cities told of in
the 'Arabian Nights'; yet the genie of all this would be naught but
the intelligence of man working in unison."[98] As a symbol of
united intelligence, Gillette offered a genie which he named
"Man Corporate" (figure 13). Gillette's colossal genie holds the
earth as if it were a baseball. Like the mural in the Schoellkoph
Power Station, this is a representation of the transformation of

13. "Man Corporate." From King Camp Gillette, *World
Corporation* (Boston: New England News Company, 1910),
opposite p. 94.

man through the transformation of nature. The symbolism is
clear: Man Corporate can take the world in the palm of his hand
and make anything of it he wishes.

Closely related to the new civilization's aesthetic appeal was its
appeal to imagination: it offered a chance to start over. Like a
new world or a virgin land, the new civilization was something to
be imagined. Gillette implored his reader: "Shut your eyes, and
imagine for a moment the whole expanse of these United States

swept clean of cities, towns, villages, farm-houses, country roads, fences and railroads." Then he instructed the reader to hold "this virgin field" before the "mind's eye" and consider whether it would be better to scatter towns, industries and population throughout this land or to gather them all together into one perfect, beautiful and rational central city.[99]

For Gillette himself, the idea of Metropolis had come in a flash of imagination, a vision. He seemed to believe that for anyone to become committed to the World Corporation, they too would have to suddenly recognize its truth and undergo a conversion. In *The Human Drift*, Gillette offered a fictional interview with a millionaire who has just transferred all of his assets to the World Corporation. "When the truth was finally impressed upon me," the millionaire tells us in language reminiscent of classical conversion narratives, "I felt like a man who had always walked in darkness, but who had suddenly found the light."[100]

Gillette believed that if his plan "could be understood by the masses, enthusiasm would amount to such a pitch in the excitement and desire to see 'Metropolis' completed that millions would enlist their services" on a voluntary basis. "Once let humanity grasp the idea of a great central city, and a future of material equality," Gillette proclaimed, "and every mind would be focused on one spot. . . . The city would actually spring into existence." Metropolis was literally to be imagined into existence: "We have found Aladdin's lamp," he continued; "let us profit by its possession."[101]

Metropolis was a vision. Physical separation from Niagara had allowed earlier travelers to picture the falls yet to be viewed as an overwhelming sight. Gillette placed his vision in the future, where temporal distance allowed him to imagine Metropolis as the heart of a perfect civilization.

Gillette's scheme obviously failed. Even his offer of a million dollars to entice Teddy Roosevelt to accept the presidency of the World Corporation met with rejection. His imagined future apparently inspired only a few. Yet those who initiated successful projects had similar, if less extreme, visions of the future. Although their visions had a considerable effect upon the landscape of Niagara Falls, it would be incorrect, to say that they imagined the future into existence. For the Niagara Falls they helped to create is far different from the one they imagined.

In 1895 the entrepreneur and inventor Leonard Henkle released another imaginative but quixotic proposal to develop Niagara Falls.[102] He envisioned a lavish palace of gigantic proportions stretching across the entire width of the Niagara River just above the crest of the falls. Henkle's intention was "to combine the most imposing grandeur of art with the natural beauty of Niagara Falls."[103] The building was to be a half-mile in length and not less than forty-six stories. He called it the "Great Dynamic Palace and International Hall."

Henkle planned to utilize all of the water flowing beneath this structure for generating electricity, believing that there would be enough power to supply all the needs of every city in the United States and Canada. With the receipts from the sale of this power, Henkle intended to finance two additional undertakings. First, he planned to construct a large fleet of steamships to sail out of the St. Lawrence to "every port in the world." Second, he proposed to build two four-track transcontinental railroads, one from British Columbia to the St. Lawrence, and the other from California to Maine. These two railroads were to cross at Niagara—in fact, they were to cross right inside the Dynamic Palace; the section above the turbines was designed to be a massive railway tunnel.

The floors above this tunnel would house manufacturing and commercial establishments. Henkle reserved the forty-sixth floor for an enormous "International Hall" with room for 70,000 people. It was to be "the most beautiful place on earth." He envisioned it as a kind of United Nations Headquarters. Each nation was to have a representative and a special place in the hall. Here, Henkle hoped, people would learn that there is only "one humanity, one country, one religion and one common ultimate destiny for man." Like Gillette, Henkle imagined an orderly future from which chaos and superstition had been eliminated. The "Great Dynamic Palace and International Hall" was to embody moral as well as material progress. "The nations of the world," Henkle proclaimed, "will be welcomed to assemble in this hall, to be taught to cease the conflicts of war and love one another. The social distinctions between poverty and wealth shall therein be destroyed."[104]

Although Henkle commissioned a very detailed set of architectural plans, his proposal remained permanently on the drawing board.

After the turn of the century, many continued to see an expansive future for Niagara Falls. A. Howell Van Cleve, for instance, argued in 1903 that the "greater Buffalo" area would become "the great manufacturing center of the land" because of the

> mighty giant delivering the fruits of his labors to her very doors. . . . The fable of the rainbow has come true, and the shimmering bow that ever spans Niagara's gorge holds at either end the hoarded wealth of the ages which will be poured into the lap of the Queen City of the nation.[105]

In 1912 Garnault Agassiz predicted that the Niagara Frontier would "become one day the greatest manufacturing center in the world." For Agassiz, the development of Niagara signified the conquest of American Nature:

> Gone is the Indian's superstition, the red man's impotency— terrible no more is the "Spirit of Niagara," ominous no longer its voice. Where stood the Indian maid we now see in phantom a thousand temples of industry; where rode the mist, a cloud as of smoke wafted toward the setting sun; where rested the rainbow, the bridge that points man across the great divide.[106]

Clearly Agassiz believed that humanity's growing power over nature promised a world that was better in every way. In the great future city he envisioned at Niagara, the superstitious reverence for nature would be replaced by a reverence for humanity's own creations—the "thousand temples of industry."

Professor Thomas H. Norton suggested a new hydroelectric scheme in 1916. He proposed to turn the falls completely off for the greater portion of each day, using the power to operate a vast industrial city at Niagara. And for the several remaining hours each day, Norton planned to let the falls flow without any diversion. But he hoped to capture much of this lost energy with "a gigantic system of scaffolds" and overshot wheels placed inconspicuously behind the falls. This scheme, Norton believed, "would mean the creation of an industrial metropolis, surpassing any now existing on the face of the globe. . . . Industries of the most varied nature . . .—all dependent upon electric current—would gravitate to this point. It would become in very truth—perhaps in name—the electropolis of America."[107] Professor Norton's plan was the last serious proposal of this grandiose kind. It soon became obvious that the power of Niagara was indeed limited and was not sufficient to create the world's greatest industrial center. Moreover, its power was transmissible.

Before turning to some of the more disquieting visions of Niagara's future, we need to consider a transitional figure: H. G. Wells. When he visited Niagara Falls in 1906, Wells was profoundly caught up in the excitement of technological progress, but he was also afflicted with nagging doubts. In his 1907 volume, *The Future in America,* Wells published an account of his visit under the title, "The End of Niagara."[108]

For Wells, the natural splendor of the falls had been "long since destroyed beyond recovery by the hotels, the factories, the power-houses, the bridges and tramways and hoardings that arose around it." Yet, looking up at the rapids above the falls, he saw "a limitless ocean" that "gripped the imagination." Still, "the real interest of Niagara for me," he wrote, "was not in the waterfall but in the human accumulations about it," for "they stood for the future." Certainly most of these accumulations were "extremely defiling and ugly." But, for Wells, they represented only "the first slovenly onslaught of mankind's expansion, the pioneers' camp of the human growth process."[109]

The dynamos and turbines of the Niagara Falls Power Company were "greater and more beautiful" than any "accidental" natural phenomenon because they were "will made visible." They were "clean" and "noiseless." Descending into the wheel-pit, Wells found "an almost cloistered quiet about its softly humming turbines." They were "noble masses of machinery" that engendered "irresistible forces." They had sprung full-grown from "speculative, foreseeing and endeavouring" brains; "first was the word and then these powers." In this power station, it was almost as if the irresistible power of nature could be held in the palm of one's hand, as Gillette's "Man Corporate" held the globe: "The dazzling clean switch-board, with its little handles and levers, is the seat of empire over more power than the strength of a million disciplined, unquestioning men." Contemplating this machinery touched off Wells's imagination; he "fell into a day-dream of the coming power of men":

> For surely the greatness of life is still to come, it is not in such accidents as mountains or the sea. . . . All the natural beauty in the world is only so much material for the imagination and the mind. . . . Man lives to make. . . . And what a world he will make—after a thousand years or so![110]

Wells believed "in the future of mankind," but he believed "passionately, as a doubting lover believes in his mistress." He was willing to forgive the present if the future was to be beautiful and orderly. It was "altogether well" that Niagara would soon come to an end if its waters "should rise again in light and power, . . . in cities and palaces and the emancipated souls and hearts of men." But Wells was not entirely convinced that this would happen:

> One feels that all the power that throbs in the copper cables below may end at last in turning great wheels for excursionists, stamping out aluminum "fancy" ware, and illuminating night advertisements for drug shops and music halls. I had an afternoon of busy doubts. . . .[111]

Wells expressed the vision of future progress more articulately than perhaps any other visitor to Niagara, yet he also harbored doubts about what kind of world humanity's new mastery over nature would produce. As we shall see, a mere two years after his visit to Niagara, these doubts coalesced into a very bleak picture of the future—and particularly of Niagara's role in that future.

Before World War I, most who spoke of the future in connection with Niagara Falls believed that the human race was progressing and would continue to progress in almost every way. But a few writers, particularly after 1900, made Niagara the focus of extremely pessimistic visions of the future. There was at least one precedent for this: throughout the nineteenth century, a number of traditional Christians had described Niagara as a herald of the Apocalypse. While gazing at the falls, their thoughts had turned to the terrifying future events predicted in Revelations.[112] For a Christian, it was possible to believe that human progress was irrelevant, whereas for others, visible progress itself—particularly industrial and mechanical progress—raised doubts about the future.

These doubts found at least two channels of expression in the industrialized world. First, there was the British tradition of social and cultural criticism of the new industrial order. This tradition had originated about 1800 and included such figures as William Cobbett, Robert Owen, and John Stuart Mill. We might also include several novels from the mid-nineteenth century, such as Mrs. Gaskell's *Mary Barton* (1848), Charles Dickens's *Hard Times* (1854), Benjamin Disraeli's *Sybil* (1845), and George Eliot's *Felix Holt* (1886). One finds in Raymond Williams's study, *Culture and Society: 1780–1950,* a detailed examination of this important current in British thinking.[113] In the literature of Niagara Falls, this tradition is represented by Thomas Carlyle's 1867 book, *Shooting Niagara: And After?*[114]

Futuristic fiction formed a second channel of expression for doubts about the future. Whereas optimism prevailed in the genre, at least until World War I, the seeds of dystopia were present even in the nineteenth century. In *The Coming Race* (1871), Edward George Bulwar-Lytton described a technically advanced society whose inhabitants lived in peace and luxury, yet were deeply unhappy in their perfect world. H. G. Wells, in *The Time Machine* (1895), depicted a similar future that had come about because "the work of ameliorating the conditions of life— the true civilizing process that makes life more and more secure—had gone on steadily to a climax. One triumph of a united humanity over Nature had followed another."[115] The "odd consequence"—as Wells called it—of this progress had been a pitifully enfeebled race. In the following pages we shall examine two novels, one by Jules Verne and the other by H. G. Wells, that make Niagara the focus of an alarming future. Both appeared in the first decade of this century and hence provide early examples of fearful visions of the future.

When Thomas Carlyle published *Shooting Niagara: And After?* in 1867, he had become thoroughly disenchanted with the whole direction taken by the modern world, and particularly England. A future loomed that would be like a fall over Niagara's brink, and after the "immortal smash,"[116] Carlyle could only see chaos. Niagara served as an image of a break in the stream of time—a break that separated the future world from the present one. At the same time, it was a perfect symbol for impending disaster.

Carlyle, both creating and reflecting a tendency of his time, had long criticized the nineteenth century as a "Mechanical Age," an age in which "nothing is . . . done directly, or by hand; all is by rule and calculated contrivance." The deeper problem, for Carlyle, was this:

> Not the external and physical alone is now managed by machinery, but the internal and spiritual also. . . . The same habit regulates not our modes of action alone, but our modes of thought and feeling. Men have grown mechanical in head and heart, as well as in hand. They have lost faith in individual endeavour, and in natural force of any kind.[117]

In his later writings, Carlyle began to associate democracy with the mechanical culture that he later dubbed "industrialism." *Shooting Niagara* was a response to attempts to extend suffrage in Great Britain—attempts, in Carlyle's opinion, that were a prescription for chaos. Complete democracy could only release the debasing force of individualism by which all Englishmen would be free "to follow each his own nose." Carlyle saw "nothing but vulgarity" in the "people's expectations"; they were only enthusiastic about "the appetites of their own huge belly, and the readiest method of assuaging these." The idea of extending suffrage to the masses was dangerous:

> It accelerates notably what I have long looked upon as inevitable;—pushed us at once into the Niagara Rapids: irresistibly propelled, with ever-increasing velocity, we shall now arrive; who knows how soon![118]

Carlyle could imagine only one way to avoid Niagara's brink: to give power to the "noble Few"—men who still could wield "natural force," men of wisdom and foresight. At times, Carlyle appealed to poets and men of learning, and at other times to the aristocracy itself and even to captains of industry. He believed that society could approach perfection; it could replace "unspeakable Chaos" with "Cosmos."[119] But for the pessimistic Carlyle this was not very likely. The future, in his view, harbored a great precipice.

Niagara Falls plays a crucial role in Jules Verne's futuristic tale, *The Master of the World* (1905).[120] The future that Verne described bears little resemblance to the one that Carlyle feared, but it is equally foreboding. Danger in Verne's world does not come from the masses but from a highly intelligent man, a Carlylian figure with great "natural force," named Robur.

Robur had also been the protagonist in Verne's 1886 novel, *Robur, the Conqueror* in which he had been a brilliant scientist and inventor who had wisely chosen to withhold "the secret of his invention" for fear that it would "greatly change the social and political conditions of the world." The world was not ready for the future, Robur had concluded; nations were "not yet fit for union." In the conclusion of this first book, Verne described his protagonist with these words: "Robur is the science of the future. Perhaps the science of to-morrow! Certainly the science that will come."[121] The man of science in this story is a man with a balanced view, a wise man.

In *The Master of the World,* Robur returns as a mad scientist with a powerful new invention. This was Verne's final book, published in the year of his death. Throughout his long and productive career, Verne perhaps had done more than any of his contemporaries to make the future seem exciting. But, as his life neared its end, he apparently was having some apprehensions about the future.

Robur's new invention first appears on the highways of Pennsylvania as a vehicle capable of speeds over 150 mph. After terrorizing pedestrians and motorists throughout the United States for several weeks, Robur demonstrates that his vehicle is also a boat that can travel at similar speeds on the surface of the Atlantic. Finally, the new vehicle appears once again, but this time as a submarine in a small lake in Kansas. When the governments of the world make public offers to the owner of the mysterious machine to "name the terms" upon which he will sell, Robur replies with an arrogant letter:

> The invention will remain my own, and I shall use it as pleases me. With it, I hold control of the entire world, and there lies no force within the reach of humanity which is able to resist me, under any circumstances whatsoever.[122]

The letter is signed "Master of the World."

As the story reaches its climax, Robur's luck finally seems to be running out. American gunboats pursue his ship, which he has named the *Terror,* into the eastern end of Lake Erie. When he attempts to dive, the submarine apparatus malfunctions and he is forced into the Niagara River. The gunboats drive the *Terror* into the rapids. But just as it approaches the brink, we learn that it can also fly (figure 14). The scene is narrated by a captive on board the *Terror:*

> The sun has set, and through the twilight the moon's rays shone upon us from the south. The speed of our craft, doubled by the speed of the current, was prodigious! In another moment, we should plunge into that black hollow which forms the very center of the Canadian Falls. With an eye of horror, I saw the shores of Goat Island flashed by, then came the Isles of the Three Sisters, drowned in the spray of the abyss. . . . Suddenly a sharp noise was heard from the mechanism which throbbed within our craft. The long gangways folded back on the sides of the machine spread out like wings, and at the moment when the Terror reached the very edge of the falls, she arose into space, escaping from the thundering cataract in the center of a lunar rainbow.[123]

Couched in accumulated symbolism, this moment is the climax of the book. Ascending from Niagara's brink, Robur has passed over to that future where human control is complete. He has defied nature and proven himself "mightier than the elements";

14. "The Escape from Niagara." From Jules Verne, *The Master of the World,* in *Works of Jules Verne,* ed. Charles F. Horne (New York: Vincent Parke and Company, 1911), opposite p. 224.

"earth, air and water combined to offer him an infinite field where none might follow him!"[124]

Yet Verne clearly did not view Robur's new power over nature favorably. It is now an arrogant, dangerous power with which Robur intends "to enslave the entire world." Indeed, we find out a few pages later that Robur's arrogance has become a fatal obsession. When the *Terror* approaches a violent hurricane in the Gulf of Mexico. Robur howls at the storm, like Ahab to the white whale: "I, Robur! Robur!—The Master of the World!" A dive beneath the sea could protect the *Terror* from the hurricane, but Robur will not bend to any force. Again, the captive describes the action:

> The great wings shot out, and the airship rose as it had risen above the falls of Niagara. But if on that day it had escaped the might of the cataract, this time it was amidst the might of the hurricane that we attempted our insensate flight.[125]

Robur directs his machine "towards the very center of the storm," where a flash of lightning sends him crashing to his death.

H. G. Wells at times praised the growth of human mastery over nature; at other times, he saw the seeds of disaster in this new power. As we have seen, when he visited Niagara Falls in 1906, Wells described the new turbines as "noble masses of machinery," but he also voiced some doubts about the uses to which the electrical power might be put. Two years after this visit, Wells used Niagara Falls as the stage for a world cataclysm in his novel, *The War in the Air*.[126] The cataclysm results from rapid technological advances that the nations of the world are ill-prepared to accommodate.

The War in the Air projects a future that appears at first like a continuation of a long historical trend:

> For three hundred years and more . . . Europeanized civilization had been in progress: towns had been multiplying, populations increasing, values rising, new countries developing; thought, literature, knowledge unfolding and spreading. It seemed but a part of the process that every year the instruments of war were vaster and more powerful, and that armies and explosives outgrew all other things.[127]

The most important development is the airship which frees humans from an immemorial natural limitation, a liberty they are not prepared to handle.

The Future of Niagara

The nations of the world proceed to build colossal air fleets. It appears, in the beginning, that the German fleet is most powerful. The leader, Prince Karl Albert, who is known as the "German Alexander," directs his fleet across the Atlantic to invade the United States. He begins by leveling New York City. Next, he proceeds to Niagara to establish a fortress where he can take advantage of the "enormous power works."[128] The Germans force all inhabitants from the area and then bomb away every structure within a perimeter of ten miles around the falls. The purpose of this is to remove any cover that might aid an American force attempting a surface attack. Unfortunately for the Germans, the attack comes from the air and it is not the Americans who launch it.

Japan and China form an alliance known as the "Confederation of East Asia" and begin to assemble a massive air fleet. At the climax of the book, the Asian fleet crosses the Pacific and advances on Niagara. When the two fleets clash over the skies of Niagara Falls, the Asians get the better of the fighting. The German flagship is downed in the upper rapids and plunges over the cataract (figure 15). As it whirls "like a huge empty sack," Wells explains that

> it meant—what did it mean?—the German air-fleet, . . . the prince, Europe, all things stable and familiar, . . . the forces that had seemed indisputably victorious. And it went down the rapids like an empty sack and left the visible world to Asia, to yellow people beyond Christendom, to all that was terrible and strange![129]

Although the conflict quickly spreads to the entire Great Lakes region and then across most of the continent, it is still called the "Battle of Niagara." Like a vortex, the battle continues to widen until it has engulfed the entire world. The Asians invade Europe and, just when it appears that they will be victorious, their massive underclasses revolt. Similar upheavals strike on the Indian subcontinent and throughout the Muslim world. "And now the whole fabric of civilization was bending and giving, and dropping to pieces and melting in the furnace of the war." The Babylonian and Roman empires "had rotted and

15. "The airship staggered to the crest of the Fall—and
vanished in a desperate leap." H. G. Wells, *The War in the Air*
(London: George Bell & Sons, 1908), opposite p. 227.

crumbled down, the Europeanized civilization was, as it were,
blown up." The collapse comes "like a fall over a cliff," while
"everywhere were men and women perceiving this, and struggling desperately to keep, as it were, a hold upon the edge of the
cliff."[130]

Within five years, the disintegration is complete. Every airship
is destroyed and every nation is reduced to chaos. The people of

both the New World and the Old revert to a savage, primitive existence. Wells summed up the story with these comments:

> For a time it had seemed that by virtue of machines and scientific civilization, Europe was to be lifted out of this perpetual round of animal drudgery, and that America was to evade it very largely from the outset. And with the smash of the high and dangerous and splendid edifice of mechanical civilization that had arisen so marvelously, back to the land came the common man, back to the manure.[131]

Today we can imagine a future that is worse than this; we can even imagine no future at all. But in 1908 this was a very gloomy picture indeed.

Niagara was a fitting setting for *The War in the Air* because the story turns ironically on the theme of the human struggle for mastery over nature. Wells and many of his contemporaries saw in the landscape of Niagara a prime example of this struggle. To most, the struggle seemed nearly over; humans had won. Wells was one of the few at this time who could imagine a different outcome: greater technological power, instead of bringing release from the struggle against nature, might in the end force humans to accept the "hard struggle against nature for food" as "the chief interest of their lives."[132] In Wells's story, the fact that humans had not won the struggle first becomes clear in the striking image of the German flagship being carried over the falls.

The unexpected catastrophes of the First World War dealt a severe blow to optimistic images of the future. Centuries of assumed progress had culminated in an unparalleled display of brutality. One immediate consequence of the war, I. F. Clarke points out, was a bifurcation between the predictions of technical forecasters and those of literary foreseers. The forecasters continued to look for new patterns of development, but the foreseers could no longer accept the proposition that "more technology and more organization must lead to a better society."[133] The idea of progress suffered a further succession of blows in the twentieth century: the Depression of the 1930s, the rise of fascism, the Second World War, the Holocaust, and the Bomb. Dystopias replaced utopias. Yet one might argue that no age has been more interested in the future than our own. The spectrum of futures we can imagine is immense. At one end is the popular literature of science fiction which has expanded steadily since the 1930s. I. F. Clarke argues that stories of space travel "compose the favorite myth in the popular literature of our time."[134] At the other end of the spectrum are ubiquitous images of thermonuclear destruction.

At Niagara Falls, nonetheless, an optimistic view both of the future and of technological progress persisted even after the Great War. By this time, Niagara's reputation as a symbol of progress had been overshadowed by developments elsewhere, which may explain why novelists ceased to use it as a stage for futuristic dramas. Nevertheless, at least one tale of the future is set at Niagara Falls during the postwar period. It appeared in a new popular medium, the comic strip. It demonstrates that even fiction of this sort could no longer sanguinely present progress as inevitable; but perhaps it also shows that the popular audience for this fiction was not yet willing to give up hope in the possibility of progress.

The original story of *Buck Rogers in the Twenty-Fifth Century* first appeared as a comic strip in 1929, written by Philip Nowlan and illustrated by Dick Calkins.[135] At the beginning of the story, Buck Rogers inhales some sinister gas in a cave near Pittsburgh and falls into a deep sleep that lasts 500 years. He awakens to find that North America has been invaded by "mongols," a technologically superior race armed with devastating airships and disintegrator rays. The original Americans have been reduced to a single stronghold: Niagara City. Here, the falling water powers a shield of fire, making Niagara "the one spot in all North America safe from mongol air raids" (figure 16).

The story presents an equivocal view of technological progress. In the hands of the mongols, advanced technology is a destructive force, yet machines have made the mongols soft and effete. The Americans, in explicitly moral contrast, continue to work eight hours a day instead of letting machines lighten their load "because people must work or civilization would decay."[136] On the other hand, nature is completely dominated at Niagara

16. Buck Rogers arrives at the capital city.
Robert C. Dille, *The Collected Works of Buck
Rogers in the 25th Century* (New York:
Chelsea House, 1969), strip #91, p. 23.

17. Niagara City and Falls. Robert C. Dille, *The Collected Works of Buck Rogers in the 25th Century* (New York: Chelsea House, 1969), strip #129, p. 33.

City. With no lawns or trees, it is a landscape entirely of human design, almost as extreme as Gillette's Metropolis (figure 17). Moreover, it is the Americans' technological ingenuity in tapping the power of Niagara that preserves their freedom. Indeed, as the story unfolds, the Americans are able to strike back from their impenetrable fortress and eventually win back the continent. The sublimated moral tale of Buck Rogers begins as a story of future disaster but ends by affirming that progress will ultimately abide.

After World War I, many people continued to express confidence that the story of Niagara's future would be one of great progress. The future would be better, they believed, because of increasing control over nature and over the forces of social and political chaos.

In June 1925, a week-long "Power and Progress Exposition" was held at Niagara Falls to commemorate the thirtieth anniversary of electrical power transmission to Buffalo. Local promoters wanted to dedicate a new battery of permanent lights for night illumination of the falls,[137] and they wished to observe what they considered moral progress on the Niagara frontier. The citizens of the two nations had lived together in peace for over 100 years. The lieutenant governor of Canada met the lieutenant governor of New York State halfway across the bridge for a "Peace Ceremony." As evidence of the growing "brotherhood" between the two nations, observers noted that the mayor of Niagara Falls, New York, had been born in Canada and was a naturalized American citizen, while the mayor of Niagara Falls, Ontario, had been born in the United States and was a naturalized Canadian citizen.[138] The exposition was capped off with an enormous fireworks display and the crowning of the "Queen of Power."[139]

The city leaders of Niagara Falls, New York, decided the following year to make the celebration an annual event to be called the "Festival of Lights." The 1926 version included a large parade and the crowning of "Queen Electra." The festival began to grow, and in 1927, the ceremonies were broadcast throughout New York State. The 1928 parade included 125 floats. But the peak year was certainly 1929, when the festival drew over 200,000 visitors to commemorate the fiftieth anniversary of the first electric lighting of Niagara Falls. Local leaders created a "golden pathway" in the city streets by tinting the streetlights yellow, and a broadcaster described the event as he stood on the bridge with one foot in each nation.[140] The 1930 festival was also a great success, but the worsening depression brought the tradition to an abrupt halt.

Just after World War II, the peaceful border at Niagara Falls helped to inspire another expression of optimism about the future. The war and the atomic bomb had so changed the international order that some saw a chance for a new beginning. The old hope for the unity of humankind was revived, the most concrete result of which was the establishment of the United Nations. At Niagara, as noted earlier, local leaders on both sides of the river believed that Navy Island, which sits in Canadian waters just above the falls, would be a perfect site for the new United Nations headquarters.[141] The promoters who submitted the Navy

Island proposal were apparently unaware that both Gillette and Henkle had imagined Niagara as the focal point of a united humanity fifty years before them. When the United Nations decided to locate their headquarters in the United States, local promoters offered a site on Grand Island, just upstream from Navy Island; Grand Island became one of the final four sites considered.[142]

Perhaps the clearest expression of continuing belief in progress at Niagara has been the willingness to push on with the work envisioned by men like Love and Gillette and initiated by such firms as the Niagara Falls Power Company. There has been a will to develop ever greater amounts of power at Niagara—a will to take nature's power in hand with the confidence that a better future can thereby be created. This trend has met little organized resistance. The international treaty of 1909 had limited total diversion by the power plants to 56,000 cubic feet per second— about one-quarter of Niagara's average flow of 202,000 c.f.s. Because of power demands brought on by World War II, additional diversions were authorized in 1940, 1941, 1944, and 1948,[143] raising the total allowable level of diversion to 89,000 c.f.s. In 1950, a new international treaty simply specified that 100,000 c.f.s. must flow over the falls during the daylight hours of the tourist season and 50,000 c.f.s. at all other times.[144] This meant that the power plants were allowed to divert approximately two-thirds of the normal yearly flow. Following the agreement, massive new hydroelectric plants were built on both sides of the river; they now have the capacity to use almost 85 percent of Niagara's average flow.[145]

Withdrawing the volumes of water permitted under the 1950 treaty would have thinned the flank areas of the Horseshoe Falls to a trickle and left the American Falls virtually dry. To prevent this, the flank areas were sculpted out to provide an even flow, and a large control structure was installed to divert water toward the American Falls.[146]

After World War I, industry also expanded greatly at Niagara Falls, so that by 1940, cheap electricity had enabled the area to become the world's largest producer of electrochemicals. The electrochemical industry had been created virtually out of nothing. Nonexistent before 1900, this industry produced insecticides, medicines, and hundreds of other products merely by shooting electrical currents through brine and other solutions. During the 1940s and 1950s, publications of the chemical companies, and even professional journals of chemical engineering, described the industry as magically expansive.[147] A 1954 pamphlet issued by the Union Carbide and Carbon Corporation, for instance, concludes with this paean to chemical progress:

> The chemical genie is creating new products faster than the historian can record them. The development of new products has been so tremendous that more than half the output of the leading chemical companies today is devoted to products which were unknown only 15 years ago. Such advances have contributed to a more abundant life for us all.[148]

By the mid-1960s, however, Niagara Falls was running out of electricity to feed the "chemical genie." To remedy this situation, a planning report by the Hudson Institute suggested that a nuclear power plant should be built at Niagara Falls to attract more industry. The authors of the report argued that such a plant would be "right in the tradition of the area."[149] Finally, in 1965 a group of local leaders, hoping to attract a new kind of industrial development, submitted a proposal to the Atomic Energy Commission for a "National Accelerator Laboratory" at Niagara Falls.[150]

Why did so many people, particularly between 1890 and 1910, imagine Niagara Falls as an important focus of the future? One reason was that the novelty of the future was almost universally associated with technological progress, with humanity's struggle for dominance over nature. This was true for those who considered the new technological power good as well as for those who thought it evil. As Niagara had long been seen as a symbol of nature, and as there had been continuous attempts to harness its waterpower in the late nineteenth century, the struggle to overcome nature—and therefore to usher in the future—found a locus both symbolic and literal at Niagara Falls.

There was a second reason why people's imaginations turned

to the future at the falls. As we have seen, during the long period before Niagara became accessible, an image of a stupendous waterfall had developed from afar. Then, in the nineteenth century many people began to associate Niagara with the distant past of primeval nature and the mysterious world of the afterlife. Each of these was a remote realm whose nature, like that of a distant waterfall, could only be imagined. Those who imagined the future at Niagara near the turn of the century were extending an old cluster of images in a new direction.

Does the imagined future Niagara bear any relation to the Niagara one finds today? Niagara Falls is not North America's greatest metropolis, but neither is it a placid national park. The falls sits at the center of a landscape that has been vigorously developed. Development, of course, was only possible because of Niagara's location and the timing of certain technological innovations, but the evidence I have presented here suggests an additional factor. The image of Niagara's future presented in the utopian schemes of the 1890s has not been realized, yet that image gave momentum to greater and greater exploitation of Niagara's power. As those who suggested a nuclear power plant for Niagara commented, development has been "right in the tradition of the area." The old image of a stupendous, immeasurable waterfall lured Gillette, Love, Henkle, and the leaders of the Niagara Falls Power Company. Niagara was vigorously developed not because developers thought so little of the falls' natural splendor, but rather because they thought so much of it.

Those who imagined a disastrous future for Niagara Falls were, on the whole, wrong. There has been no catastrophic battle here; neither have people reverted to savagery. Yet there is some irony in what has become of Love's 1893 canal. The Hooker Chemical Company turned the mile-long trench into a waste disposal site. By 1953 the district had become residential, and Hooker "donated" the site for the construction of a public school and playground. When chemicals began leaking and causing serious health problems in the late 1970s, the Love Canal became the infamous site of America's first toxic waste disaster.[151] Love's canal, instead of leading to the perfect future city, has become a place that, as far as human habitation is concerned, may have no future at all, and the very term, Love Canal, has come to symbolize technological disaster. The Love Canal fiasco is an example of how human mastery over nature—human technological power—can become a destructive force.

The jury is still out on Niagara's future—indeed, on humanity's future. Perhaps the one conclusion we can draw from the history of Niagara Falls is that the *way* we imagine the future may be very important.

CONCLUSION

*A*fter a 1791 visit to Niagara Falls, the romantic young Frenchman Chateaubriand asked:

> What meaning has a cascade which falls eternally in the unfeeling sight of heaven and earth if human nature be not there with its destinies and misfortunes? To be steeped in this solitude of water and mountains and not to know with whom to speak of that great spectacle! To have the waves, the rocks, the woods, the torrents to one's self alone![1]

There is a clear note of ambivalence here: in spite of his words, Chateaubriand's exhilaration bursts through; for him, the loneliness and inaccessibility of the falls enshrine its grandeur. Within a few short decades, Niagara's visitors would be envious of Chateaubriand's experience at the cataract. "Blessed were the wanderers of old," wrote Hawthorne in 1834, "who heard its deep roar, sounding through the woods."[2] In another way, however, Chateaubriand was right: Niagara has no pure, natural meaning unrelated to "human nature," with its "destinies and misfortunes." Whatever meanings it has, have emerged through human involvement with the place.

It would seem that for many visitors—especially those who came in the nineteenth century—Niagara's meaning was essentially individual: a personal encounter with nature, death, or God. The individual experience at Niagara may be likened to the vision quest of many native North American societies; although the quest is an individual experience, its practice is a collective cultural creation. Individual encounters with Niagara, taken together, also form a cultural pattern. The whole phenomenon of Niagara Falls—its idealization, its great international attraction as a travel destination—must be understood primarily as a creation of Europeans and their North American descendents. Certain conditions internal to European culture—among them, the weakening of traditional religious awe and the emergence of the new bourgeois class—conspired to make appealing the exotic, the other. By the early nineteenth century, Niagara Falls had become a kind of lightning rod, appropriating to itself a powerful aura of otherness. For many Europeans, Niagara was more than a mere cataract falling in the wilderness; it was a thing unconstrained by the limits of the ordinary world, a thing whose nature could be apprehended only with imagination. It was construed as infinite, bottomless, sacred. To envision Niagara Falls this way was a collective act of imagination—one might say, a collective delusion. When the actual experience at Niagara did not match the expectations engendered by this delusion, many were disappointed. But some, like Hawthorne, were able to recapture Niagara's otherness through a new act of imagination.

The preceding chapters investigated four thematic versions of Niagara's otherness. In each, the falls is a place of transformation, a kind of portal between this world and some mysterious other one: the exotically remote, the afterlife, nature, or the future. Not only are these *meanings* a collective cultural creation, so indeed is the *place* itself—its landscape, its institutions, its social role, its history. The making of Niagara Falls, it should now be clear, is intimately connected with the meaning of Niagara Falls. The most striking example of this connection is the industrial development itself. The idealization of Niagara as the indelimitable "other" made the place irresistible to industrialists. For otherwise hardheaded businessmen, an almost magical progress appeared possible because Niagara's power seemed beyond measurement.

This view of Niagara—and indeed of the entire natural world—as an exhaustless storehouse wholly separate from ourselves promised endless industrial expansion. But stubborn realities will sometimes fail to be overcome by the strength of our human desires and visions. The 1957 visitor who came to Niagara Falls claiming to be God discovered this when he attempted to walk on the water near the cataract's brink.[3] In a similar way, the Love Canal disaster was one of the signal events that shocked us into awareness of certain basic principles of ecology. The natural world cannot supply us with unlimited resources and accept endless amounts of our industrial wastes. There is an interlocking web that sustains all life on this planet. Human beings are not separate and exceptional: like rabbits and salmon, we are vulnerable and dependent parts of the whole.

This book began with the observation that Niagara is a strange place. For the contemporary visitor, the strangeness is perhaps no longer related to the lure of some exotic otherness glimpsed through the portal of Niagara. Now it is the total gestalt of what humans have created here that seems mysterious. Today we can experience Niagara reflexively not because nature is our mirror, but because it is now unavoidably clear that we are and have always been the creators of Niagara. And what a bizarre text we have written here!

Niagara Falls was the site of great optimism about human progress, and indeed real success in the exploitation of nature's power. Here was the world's first electrical power transmission, yet here also is the Love Canal. Like the Apollo photographs taken of our fragile Earth from the immensity of deep space, the Love Canal became a harbinger of an important realization. It was one of the principal events that brought home to us the reality of our limited biological existence. That this disaster should happen at Niagara Falls is no accident, but it is uncanny that it should happen on the ruins of a utopian project. Niagara

Conclusion

Falls may no longer inspire the same awe and ecstasy it once did, but if it could inspire today's visitors to ponder the interconnectedness of all that people have thought and felt and actually created at Niagara, many might come away less than disappointed, perhaps even fascinated by the strangeness of the place.

NOTES

1. Imagining Niagara

1. H. G. Wells, *The Future in America: A Search after Realities* (Leipzig: Bernhard Tauchnitz, 1907), p. 62.

2. Frank H. Severance, *Peace Episodes on the Niagara*, Buffalo Historical Society Publications 18 (Buffalo: Buffalo Historical Society, 1914), pp. 95–112.

3. A complication first noted by the eighteenth-century Italian thinker Giambattista Vico; see Isaiah Berlin, "Vico's Concept of Knowledge," in *Against the Current: Essays in the History of Ideas* (1979; reprint ed., New York: Penguin, 1982), pp. 111–19.

4. Clifford Geertz, "Thick Description: Toward an Interpretive Theory of Culture," in *The Interpretation of Cultures: Selected Essays* (New York: Basic Books, 1973), pp. 3–30; quotation from p. 25.

5. Nathaniel Hawthorne, "My Visit to Niagara," in *Tales, Sketches and Other Papers* (Boston: Houghton, Mifflin, 1883), pp. 38–50; quotation from p. 45.

6. James K. Liston, *Niagara Falls: A Poem in Three Cantos* (Toronto: for author by J. H. Lawrence, 1843), p. 36.

7. Louis Hennepin, *Description de la Louisiane, Nouvellement Decouverte au Sud 'Ouest de la Nouvelle France . . .* (Paris: Chez la Veuve Sabastien Hure, 1683), pp. 29–30.

8. Frank H. Severance, *Studies of the Niagara Frontier*, Buffalo Historical Society Publications 15 (Buffalo: Buffalo Historical Society, 1911), p. 70. Other

general sources for general Niagara history include: Hamilton B. Mizer, *Niagara Falls: A Topical History, 1892–1932* (Lockport, N.Y.: Niagara County Historical Society, 1981); George Seibel, ed., *Niagara Falls Canada: A History* (Niagara Falls, Ontario: Kiwanis Club of Stamford, Ontario, 1967).

9. John F. Sears, *Sacred Places: American Tourist Attractions in the Nineteenth Century* (New York: Oxford University Press, 1989).

10. Elizabeth McKinsey, *Niagara Falls: Icon of the American Sublime* (Cambridge: At the University Press, 1985); Elizabeth McKinsey, "An American Icon," in *Niagara: Two Centuries of Changing Attitudes, 1697–1901,* ed. Jeremy Elwell Adamson (Washington, D.C.: The Corcoran Gallery of Art, 1985), pp. 83–101.

11. "Niagara Falls Canada: World's Most Famous Address," tourism pamphlet, n.d., p. 4; "Buffalo and Greater Niagara Vacationland," tourism pamphlet, n.d., estimates 12 million annual visitors.

12. Seibel, *Niagara Falls Canada,* p. 321.

13. McKinsey, *Niagara Falls;* Adamson, *Niagara;* Joyce Elain Sievers, "Niagara Falls: Reflections of the Landscape Sensibility in Nineteenth-Century American Painting," M.A. thesis, Illinois State University, 1980; Christopher Mulvey, *Anglo-American Landscapes: A Study of the Nineteenth-Century Anglo-American Travel Literature* (Cambridge: At the University Press, 1983); Peter Conrad, *Imagining America* (New York: Oxford University Press, 1980).

14. Marjorie Hope Nicolson, *Mountain Gloom and Mountain Glory: The Development of the Aesthetics of the Infinite* (1959; reprint ed., New York: W. W. Norton & Co., 1963).

15. Ibid., pp. 136, 143.

16. McKinsey, *Niagara Falls,* pp. 7–36.

17. Samuel H. Monk, *The Sublime: A Study of Critical Theories in XVIII-Century England* (New York: Modern Language Association of America, 1935); Walter Hipple, *The Beautiful, the Sublime, and the Picturesque in Eighteenth-Century British Aesthetic Theory* (Carbondale, Ill.: The Southern Illinois University Press, 1957); Theodore Wood, *The Word 'Sublime' and Its Context: 1650–1760* (Paris: Mouton, 1972).

18. Edmund Burke, *A Philosophical Inquiry into the Origin of Our Ideas of the Sublime and the Beautiful,* ed. J. T. Boulton (1757; reprint ed., Notre Dame, Ind.: University of Notre Dame Press, 1968).

19. Mikhail Bakhtin, *The Dialogic Imagination,* ed. Michael Holquist (Austin: University of Texas Press, 1981).

20. Michael Hoffman, *The Subversive Vision: American Romanticism in Literature* (Port Washington, N.Y.: Kennikat Press, 1972), p. 9.

21. Henry David Thoreau, *Walden and Other Writings,* ed. Brooks Atkinson (New York: Modern Library, 1950), p. 292.

22. Ralph Waldo Emerson, "The Transcendentalist" (1841), *The Collected*

Works of Ralph Waldo Emerson (Cambridge, Mass.: Harvard University Press, 1971), pp. 201–16; quotation from p. 207.

23. Herman Melville, *Moby Dick* (New York: Library Publications, 1930), p. 16.

24. Jacques Barzun, *Classic, Romantic and Modern* (Boston: Little, Brown, 1943), p. 24; W. H. Auden, *The Enchafed Flood* or *The Romantic Iconography of the Sea* (New York: Random House, 1950), p. 14; Allan Rodway, *The Romantic Conflict* (London: Chatto and Windus, 1963), p. 7; Arnold Hauser, "A Flight from Reality," in *Romanticism: Problems of Definition, Explanation, and Evaluation,* ed. John B. Halsted (Boston: D. C. Heath, 1965), pp. 67–76; quotation from p. 70.

25. F. L. Lucas, *Decline and Fall of the Romantic Ideal* (New York: Macmillan Co., 1937), pp. 51–52.

26. Auden, *Enchafed Flood,* p. 13.

27. Clarence Glacken, *Traces on the Rhodian Shore: Nature and Culture in Western Thought from Ancient Times to the End of the Eighteenth Century* (Berkeley: University of California Press, 1967), pp. 471–96.

28. Yi-Fu Tuan, "The City: Its Distance from Nature," *Geographical Review* 68(1978): 1–12.

29. Steven Mintz and Susan Kellogg, *Domestic Revolutions: A Social History of American Family Life* (New York: Free Press, 1988), p. 44.

30. Raymond Williams, *Culture and Society: 1780–1950* (New York: Columbia University Press, 1958).

31. Georg Lukacs, *Soul and Form* (Cambridge, Mass.: MIT Press, 1974), p. 55.

32. Page numbers given in text are all from Library Publications edition; see note 23, above.

33. Leo Marx, "The Machine in the Garden," in his *The Pilot and the Passenger: Essays on Literature, Technology, and Culture in the United States* (New York: Oxford University Press, 1988), pp. 113–26; quotation from p. 114.

2. *The Distant Niagara*

1. Yi-Fu Tuan, *Topophilia: A Study of Environmental Perception, Attitudes and Values* (Englewood Cliffs, N.J.: Prentice-Hall, 1974), p. 129.

2. Ibid., pp. 129–49.

3. Lewis Mumford, *The Condition of Man* (New York: Harcourt, Brace and Co., 1944), pp. 231–32.

4. Henri Baudet, *Paradise on Earth,* trans. Elizabeth Wentholt (New Haven and London: Yale University Press, 1965), p. 74.

5. John K. Wright, *Geographical Lore of the Times of the Crusades* (New York: American Geographical Society, 1925), p. 357.

6. Ibid., pp. 73, 248–50; Revelations 20:7.

7. Genesis 2:8.

8. Wright, *Lore,* pp. 71–72, 263.

9. Ibid., pp. 205, 265, 285.

10. Job 22:24.

11. Wright, *Lore,* pp. 280–81.

12. John Parker, *Discovery: Developing Views of the Earth* (New York: Charles Scribner's Sons, 1972), p. 78.

13. Ibid., p. 89.

14. John L. Allen, "Lands of Myth, Waters of Wonder: The Place of the Imagination in Geographical Exploration," in *Geographies of the Mind,* ed. David Lowenthal and Martyn Bowden (New York: Oxford University Press, 1976), p. 48.

15. Wright, *Lore,* p. 57.

16. Allen, "Lands of Myth," p. 54.

17. Howard Mumford Jones, *O Strange New World* (1952; reprint ed., New York: Viking Press, 1964), p. 4; see also P. J. Marshall and Glyndwn Williams, *The Great Map of Mankind: Perceptions of New Worlds in the Age of Enlightenment* (Cambridge, Mass.: Harvard University Press, 1982); Frederick Turner, *Beyond Geography: The Western Spirit against the Wilderness* (New York: Viking Press, 1980); Joshua C. Taylor, *America As Art* (New York: Harper & Row, 1976).

18. Jones, *O Strange New World,* pp. 3–4.

19. From his letter to Ferdinand and Isabella, written at Hispaniola during his third voyage, quoted in Jones, *O Strange New World,* p. 8.

20. Jones, *O Strange New World,* p. 33.

21. Dollier de Casson and De Brehan de Galinee, *Exploration of the Great Lakes, 1669–1670,* trans. and ed. James H. Coyne, Ontario Historical Society, Papers and Records (Toronto: The Society, 1903), 4: 38–41; reprinted in Frank H. Severance, *Studies of the Niagara Frontier,* Buffalo Historical Society Publications 15 (Buffalo: Buffalo Historical Society, 1911), p. 13.

22. Severance, *Niagara Frontier,* p. 15; see also Charles Mason Dow, ed., *Anthology and Bibliography of Niagara Falls,* 2 vols. (Albany: State of New York, 1921), 1:49.

23. Louis Hennepin, *Description de la Louisiane, Nouvellement Decouverts au Sud 'Ouest de la Nouvelle France* (Paris: Chez la Veuve Sebastien Hure, 1683).

24. Louis Hennepin, *Nouvelle Decouverte d'un Tres Grand Pays Situe dans l'Amerique* (Utrecht: Chez Guillaume Broedelet, 1697).

25. Hennepin's depiction of the falls appeared in *Nouvelle Decouverte,* 1697; see Severance, *Niagara Frontier,* pp. 118–19; and Elizabeth McKinsey, *Niagara Falls: Icon of the American Sublime* (Cambridge: Cambridge University Press, 1985), pp. 17–18.

26. See, for example, Willis Gaylord Clarke, untitled poem, quoted in

George W. Holley, *Niagara: Its History and Geology, Incidents and Poetry* (Toronto: Hunter, Rose and Co., 1872), pp. 161–62; John Edward Howell, "Niagara," in *Poems* (New York: by author, 1867), p. 222; James K. Liston, *Niagara Falls: A Poem in Three Cantos* (Toronto: for author by J. H. Lawrence, 1843), p. 36; J. C. Boonefons, *Voyage au depuis l'An 1751 a 1761,* reprinted in Severance, *Niagara Frontier,* pp. 335–39.

27. Peter Kalm, "A Letter from Mr. Kalm, a Gentleman of Sweden, Now on His Travels in America, to His Friend in Philadelphia, Containing a Particular Account of the Great Fall of Niagara, September 2, 1750," *Gentleman's Magazine* 21 (January 1751):15–19; quotation from p. 19.

28. Anthony Trollope, *North America* (London: Chapman and Hall, 1862), p. 144.

29. John C. Brainard, untitled poem, in *Poems* (Hartford: Edward Hopkins, 1842), p. 10; see also Holley, *Niagara,* p. 165; and William Dean Howells, *The Niagara Book* (Buffalo: Underhill and Nichols, 1893), pp. 138–39.

30. Mrs. A.B.M. Jameson, *Winter Studies and Summer Rambles in Canada,* 2 vols. (London: Saunders & Otley, 1838), 1: 82.

31. Nathaniel Hawthorne, "My Visit to Niagara," in *Tales, Sketches, and Other Papers* (1859; reprint ed., Boston and New York: Houghton, Mifflin and Co., 1883), pp. 42–50.

32. Hawthorne initially had envied the "wanderers of old" who had come upon Niagara with no expectations. For a detailed discussion of Hawthorne's "recovery of the sublime," see McKinsey, *Niagara Falls,* pp. 191–95.

33. James Dixon, *Personal Narrative of a Tour through a Part of the United States and Canada* (New York: Lane & Scott, 1849), p. 124.

34. Victor Turner, "The Center Out There: Pilgrim's Goal," *History of Religions* 12(1973): 191–230.

35. Thomas Grinfield, "Hymn on Niagara," in *Descriptions of Niagara,* ed. William Barham (Gravesend: The Compiler [c. 1870]), pp. 176–77; quotation from p. 177.

36. Aimery Pecaud, *Guide Du Pelerin,* quoted in Alan Kendall, *Medieval Pilgrims* (London: Wayland Publishers, 1970), p. 105.

37. Donald R. Howard, *Writers and Pilgrims: Medieval Pilgrimage Narratives and Their Posterity* (Berkeley: University of California Press, 1980), pp. 6–7.

38. C. K. Yang, quoted in Turner, "The Center Out There," p. 193; see also Victor Turner and Edith Turner, *Image and Pilgrimage in Christian Culture* (New York: Columbia University Press, 1978); Jonathan Sumption, *Pilgrimage: An Image of Medieval Religion* (Totowa, N.J.: Rowman and Littlefield, 1975); Mary Lee Nolan, "Irish Pilgrimage: The Different Tradition," *Annals,* Association of American Geographers 73(1983): 421–38.

39. Turner, "The Center Out There," p. 205.

40. Ibid., p. 204.

41. Ibid., p. 214; Kendall also describes pilgrims as crossing a limen in search of the miraculous, in *Medieval Pilgrims,* p. 17.

42. Turner, "The Center Out There," p. 210.

43. Paul Dudley, "An Account of the Falls of the River Niagara, Taken at Albany, October 10, 1721, from Monsieur Borassaw, a French Native of Canada," Royal Society of London, Philosophical Transactions, April–May 1722, pp. 69–72; see also Carl O. Sauer, "The Role of Niagara Falls in History," *Historical Outlook* 10(1919): 57–65; quotation from p. 62.

44. Sauer, "The Role of Niagara Falls," p. 62.

45. Nicholas A. Woods, *The Prince of Wales in Canada and the United States* (London: Bradbury and Evans, 1861), pp. 235–52.

46. Phillip W. Porter and Fred E. Lukermann, "The Geography of Utopia," in *Geographies of the Mind,* ed. Lowenthal and Bowden, p. 215.

47. George Houghton, "Niagara," in *Niagara and Other Poems* (Boston: Houghton, Mifflin and Co., 1882), pp. 20–21.

48. Katherine Lee Bates, "The Song of Niagara," *Canadian Magazine,* May 1910, p. 58.

49. Abraham Coles, *The Microcosm and Other Poems* (New York: D. Appleton and Co., 1881), pp. 226–35.

50. George Menzies, in *Album of the Table Rock, Niagara Falls* (Buffalo: Jewett, Thomas and Co., 1848), pp. 16–17.

51. Rev. John Dowling, in *Album of the Table Rock,* p. 32.

52. A.R.P., in *Album of the Table Rock,* pp. 40–41.

53. Archbishop John Lynch, "Pastoral Letter," reprinted in Frank H. Severance, *Peace Episodes on the Niagara,* Buffalo Historical Society Publications 18 (Buffalo: Buffalo Historical Society, 1914), p. 110; discussion of the designation, pp. 95–112.

54. Lynch, quoted in Severance, *Peace Episodes,* p. 103.

55. Unsigned, *Album of the Table Rock,* p. 44.

56. Trollope, *North America,* p. 145.

57. George Carlisle, "Two Lectures on the Poetry of Pope, and on His Own Travels in America," delivered to the Leeds Mechanics' Institution and Literary Society, December 5th and 6th, 1850 (Leeds: 1850), quoted in Dow, *Anthology* 2: 1072–73; quotation from p. 1073.

58. George Seibel, ed., *Niagara Falls Canada: A History* (Niagara Falls, Ontario: Kiwanis Club of Stamford, Ontario, 1967), pp. 292–93.

59. James C. Carter, "Oration of the Dedication of the State Reservation at Niagara, July 15, 1885," Nineteenth Annual Report of the Commissioners of the State Reservation at Niagara (Albany: State of New York, 1903), pp. 263–67, reprinted in Dow, *Anthology* 2: 1118–28; quotation from p. 1118.

60. Howard, *Writers and Pilgrims,* p. 107.

61. Seibel, *Niagara Falls,* p. 226; Gordon Donaldson, *Niagara!: The Eternal Circus* (New York: Doubleday, 1979), p. 155.

62. Donaldson, *Niagara!,* p. 240.

63. The quotations are from undated (c. 1985) promotional brochures and pamphlets with the following titles, respectively: "Circus World," "Pyramid Place," "Niagara Falls Canada," "Maple Leaf Village," "CP Hotels: Skylon."

64. John F. Sears, *Sacred Places: American Tourist Attractions in the Nineteenth Century* (New York: Oxford University Press, 1989), p. 212.

65. Turner, "The Center Out There," p. 208.

66. Ibid., p. 204.

67. Ellen K. Rothman, " 'Intimate Acquaintance': Courtship and the Transition to Marriage in America, 1770–1900," Ph.D. thesis, Brandeis University, 1981.

68. William D. Howells, *Their Wedding Journey* (Boston and New York: Houghton and Mifflin and Co., 1888), p. 319.

3. Death at Niagara

1. Margaret Fuller, *Summer on the Lakes* (1856; reprint ed., New York: Haskell House, 1970), p. 21.

2. Deborah Williams, "The Hills of Niagara," *Buffalo Courier Express,* November 28, 1976.

3. George Seibel, ed., *Niagara Falls, Canada: A History* (Niagara Falls, Ontario: Kiwanis Club of Stamford, Ontario, 1967), p. 395.

4. James Marden, *Historic Niagara Falls* (Niagara Falls, Ontario: Lindsay Press, 1932), p. 113.

5. William Dean Howells, "Avery," a poem included in *Their Wedding Journey* (Boston: James R. Osgood, 1872), p. 141; for statistics on deaths at Niagara, see Andy O'Brian, *Daredevils of Niagara* (Toronto: Ryerson Press, 1964), p. 124.

6. For example, George W. Holley, in *The Falls of Niagara* (New York: A. C. Armstrong and Son, 1883) describes 36 accidents, 12 suicides, 2 murders, 1 attempted murder, and 2 narrow escapes; S. DeVeaux, in *The Falls of Niagara* (Buffalo: William B. Hayden, 1839) describes 12 deaths; Thomas Tugby, in his *Illustrated Guide to Niagara Falls* (New York: Tugby, 1889), tells of 36 deaths; and F. H. Johnson, in his *Guide to Niagara Falls and Its Scenery* (Philadelphia: George W. Childs, 1868) describes 15 deaths.

7. Isabella Lucy Bird, *The Englishwoman in America* (1856, London; reprint ed., Toronto: University of Toronto Press, 1966), pp. 244–45; the story is also related by George W. Holley in *Niagara: Its History and Geology, Incidents and Poetry* (Toronto: Hunter, Rose and Co., 1872), pp. 123–24.

Notes to Death at Niagara

8. François Auguste René Chateaubriand, *Atala, or the Amours of Two Indians in the Wilds of America* (London: for J. Lee, 1802; first French edition: 1801).

9. James Fenimore Cooper, *The Spy: A Tale of the Neutral Ground* (1821), ed. Warren Walker (New York: Hafner, 1960).

10. The Deputy, *The Niagara Falls Detective or Solving the Whirlpool Mystery,* Old Cap. Collier Library, five-cent edition, no. 324 (New York: Munro's Publishing House, 1888); and R. W. Francis, *The Great Mystery of Niagara Falls or Detective Payne's Greatest Case,* no. 578, same series, 1895.

11. Henry Hathaway, *Niagara;* produced by Charles Brackett; written by Charles Brackett, Walter Reisch, and Richard Breen; released by 20th Century-Fox, 1953.

12. Charles Dudley Warner, *Their Pilgrimage* (New York: Harper Brothers, 1892), p. 312.

13. Mrs. Anna Jameson, *Winter Studies and Summer Rambles in Canada,* 3 vols. (London: Saunders and Otley, 1838), 2: 53.

14. James Knox Liston, *Niagara Falls: A Poem in Three Cantos* (Toronto: for author by J. H. Lawrence, 1843), p. 54.

15. W. A. Boord, F.R.G.S., *Niagara: An Appreciation* (Sydney, N.S.W.: by author, 1898), p. 4.

16. Ibid., p. 3.

17. This advertisement appeared in the guidebook, *How to See Niagara* (n.p., 1888).

18. Dr. Thomas Rolph, *A Brief Account, Together with Observations During a Visit in the West Indies, and a Tour through the United States of America, in Parts of the Years 1832–3* (Dundas, Upper Canada: Heyworth Hackstaff, 1836), p. 194.

19. "Daredevil Exploits at Niagara," a chronological listing of stunts and stunters, 1829–1933, mimeographed (Niagara Falls, N.Y., Public Library).

20. Louise Continelli, "Over and Out," *Buffalo Magazine, Buffalo News,* March 13, 1988, pp. 6–15.

21. Jean Albert Lussier tried the rubber ball device in 1928; see "Daredevil Exploits at Niagara," p. 4.

22. Jay L. V. Allen, "Permission Is 'Up in Air' for Falls High Wire Walk," *Buffalo Courier-Express,* August 13, 1974, p. 12; for a more general discussion of daredevils and their motivations, see Samuel Z. Klausner, ed., *Why Man Takes Chances: Studies in Stress-Seeking* (Garden City, N.Y.: Doubleday and Co., 1968).

23. Timothy J. Baker, "Woman Defied Falls, in '01: Leap for Lib?" *Buffalo Courier-Express,* December 29, 1975, p. 12.

24. Holley, *Niagara,* pp. 94–95; see also Roger Whitman, "Crackpots Unlimited," mimeographed (Buffalo and Erie County Historical Society, Manuscript Department), p. 6.

25. Holley, *Niagara,* pp. 95–96.

26. Ibid., p. 96.

27. Seibel, *Niagara Falls, Canada,* p. 395.

28. Continelli, "Over and Out," p. 8.

29. Diane Garey and L. R. Hott, *Niagara Falls: The Changing Nature of a New World Symbol* (Los Angeles: Direct Cinema Limited, 1985).

30. Continelli, "Over and Out," p. 8.

31. Ibid.

32. See, for example, William Barham, "Recollections of a Trip to the Falls of Niagara in September, 1845," in his *Descriptions of Niagara Selected from Various Travelers: With Original Additions* (Gravesend: The Compiler, n.d.), pp. 16–25; James Silk Buckingham, "Travels in the Eastern and Western States in 1837," in Barham, *Descriptions of Niagara,* pp. 38–46; Captain Charles Chapman, *The Ocean Waves: Travels by Land and Sea* (London: George Berridge and Co., 1875), p. 208; Abraham Coles, "A Sabbath at Niagara," in his *The Microcosm and Other Poems* (New York: D. Appleton and Co., 1881), pp. 226–34; quotation from p. 234.

33. T. R. Preston, "Remarks on Niagara," in Barham, *Descriptions,* pp. 82–86; quotations from p. 84.

34. George William Curtis, *Lotus-Eating: A Summer Book* (New York: Harper Brothers, 1852), p. 91.

35. Harriet Beecher Stowe, letter to her parents in Cincinnati, printed in Annie Fields, *Life and Letters of Harriet Beecher Stowe* (Boston: Houghton, Mifflin and Co., 1897), p. 90.

36. Sigmund Freud, *Beyond the Pleasure Principle* (1920), reprinted in *A General Selection from the Works of Sigmund Freud,* ed. John Rickman (Garden City, N.Y.: Doubleday, 1957), p. 166.

37. For accounts of the Hermit, see Holley, *Niagara,* pp. 120–21; William Fleming, *Four Days at the Falls of Niagara* (n.p.: Gillett Printer, 1835), pp. 9–12; Thomas Fowler, *The Journal of a Tour through British America to the Falls of Niagara* (Aberdeen: Lewis Smith, 1832), pp. 221–26; Merton M. Wilner, *Niagara Frontier: A Narrative and Documentary History* (Chicago: S. J. Clarke Publishing Co., 1931), pp. 761–63; Mrs. Sigourney, "The Hermit of the Falls," in *Notes on Niagara,* ed. R. Lespinasse (Chicago: R. Lespinasse, Publisher, 1884), pp. 55–59.

38. Sigourney, "Hermit of the Falls," in Barham, *Descriptions,* pp. 142–46; quotation from p. 142.

39. Fowler, *Journal of a Tour,* p. 255.

40. Fleming, *Four Days at the Falls,* p. 9.

41. Sigourney, "Hermit of the Falls," p. 56.

42. Stories of the Hermit were also standard fare in the guidebooks; the Hermit appears in at least one painting as well: Sir James Edward Alexander, "Horseshoe Falls, Niagara," 1831, depicts Abbott hanging from the beam by a

single arm before an exaggerated chasm, reproduced in Seibel, *Niagara Falls, Canada,* p. 254.

43. See, for example, Sigourney, "Hermit of the Falls."

44. James Bird, *Francis Abbott: The Recluse of Niagara, and Metropolitan Sketches* (London: Baldwin and Cradock, 1837).

45. *The History of Niagara County* (n.p.: Sanford and Co., 1898), reprinted in *Niagara Frontier: A Narrative and Documentary History,* ed. Merton M. Wilner (Chicago: S. J. Clarke, 1931), p. 763.

46. Arthur Koestler, "Where of One Cannot Speak . . .?" in Arnold Toynbee et al., *Life After Death* (New York: McGraw-Hill, 1976), pp. 238–59; quotation from p. 238.

47. Philippe Aries, *Western Attitudes toward Death: From the Middle Ages to the Present,* trans. Patricia M. Ranum (Baltimore and London: Johns Hopkins University Press, 1974), p. 13.

48. Ibid., p. 38.

49. Ibid., pp. 39–50.

50. Ibid., pp. 57, 58, 61.

51. Webb Garrison, *Strange Facts About Death* (Nashville: Arbingden, 1978), p. 124; and Geoffrey Rowell, *Hell and the Victorians* (Oxford: Clarendon Press, 1974), p. 11.

52. Rowell, *Hell,* pp. 17, 6–7, 10.

53. G. R. Thompson, ed., *The Gothic Imagination: Essays in Dark Romanticism* (Pullman: Washington State University Press, 1974).

54. G. R. Thompson, "Romanticism and the Gothic Tradition," in ibid., pp. 1–10; quotation from p. 6.

55. Harry Levin, *The Power of Blackness* (New York: Alfred A. Knopf, 1970), p. 101; Poulet cited on p. 130.

56. Cited in Panos D. Bardis, *History of Thanatology* (Washington: University Press of America, 1981), p. 72.

57. Rowell, *Hell,* p. 30.

58. Ibid., p. 212.

59. Ernest Becker, *The Denial of Death* (New York: Free Press, 1973).

60. William Chambers Wilbor, "Ode to Niagara" (Buffalo: C. E. Brinkworth, 1907).

61. Liston, *Niagara Falls,* p. 38.

62. Archbishop John Lynch, Pastoral letter, in *Peace Episodes on the Niagara,* ed. Frank H. Severance, Buffalo Historical Society Publications 18 (Buffalo: Buffalo Historical Society, 1914), pp. 104–5; see also Anonymous, "Niagara: A Poem, by a Member of the Ohio Bar" (New York: Edward O. Jenkins, 1848).

63. Anonymous, "Niagara," in *Poems of Places,* ed. Henry W. Longfellow (Boston: James R. Osgood and Co., 1879), vol. 27, *America, Middle States,* pp. 158–59; quotation from p. 158.

64. Henry James, "Niagara," in his *Portraits of Places* (Boston: Osgood, 1884), pp. 364–76; quotation from p. 372.

65. Linda de Kowalewska Fulton, *Nadia: The Maid of the Mist* (Buffalo: White-Evans-Penfold Co., 1901), pp. 22–23, 24.

66. Curtis, *Lotus-Eating,* p. 85.

67. John C. Lord, "The Genius of Niagara," in his *Occasional Poems* (Buffalo: Breed and Lent, 1869), pp. 19–22.

68. Liston, *Niagara Falls,* p. 36.

69. Nicholas A. Woods, *The Prince of Wales in Canada and the United States* (London: Bradbury and Evans, 1861), p. 239.

70. Henry Tudor, *Narrative of a Tour in North America* (London: James Duncan, 1834), p. 239.

71. For example, ibid., p. 240; Francis Lieber, *The Stranger in America, Comprising Sketches of the Manners, Society, and National Peculiarities of the United States in a Series of Letters to a Friend in Europe* (London: Richard Bentley, 1835), pp. 289–90.

72. Tudor, *Narrative of a Tour,* p. 266.

73. Henry T. Blake, "Niagara: Monarch Supreme in Nature's Glorious Realms" (Hartford: Connecticut Magazine Co., 1903).

74. George Houghton, "Niagara," in his *Niagara and Other Poems* (Boston: Houghton, Mifflin, 1882), pp. 7–28; quotation from p. 23.

75. Thomas Gold Appleton, "Niagara," in his *Faded Leaves* (Boston: Roberts Brothers, 1872), pp. 27–30; quotation from p. 30.

76. Tudor, *Narrative of a Tour,* p. 261.

77. Anthony Trollope, *North America* (New York: Harper & Brothers, 1862), p. 92.

78. See Acts 2:24 and I Peter 3:18–22.

79. "Castle Dracula," a promotional brochure; horror museums are also described in the "Niagara Falls Tour Map," (Niagara Falls, Ontario: Kiwanis Club of Stamford, Ontario), and in the promotional brochure "Niagara Falls Canada."

80. "The Haunted House and the Funhouse," promotional brochure.

81. "Ripley's Believe It or Not! Museum," promotional brochure.

82. "Niagara Serpentarium," promotional brochure.

83. "Resorts: Let's Go Again to Niagara," *Time Magazine,* June 18, 1965.

84. "Niagara Falls Canada," p. 42.

85. Sir Richard Bonnycastle, *Canada and the Canadians,* 2 vols. (London: Colburn, 1849), 1: 240.

86. William Abbott, "The World's Greatest Splash," *Collier's,* June 8, 1946.

87. "Niagara Falls Museum News," promotional brochure.

88. Fitz Hugh Ludlow, *The Hasheesh Eater* (1857, New York; reprint ed., Upper Saddle River, N.J.: Literature House, 1970), pp. 268–69; a similar story of

a fiend at the brink is told by Robert Bird, "Night on Terrapin Rocks," in his *Peter Pilgrim: or A Rambler's Recollections* (Philadelphia, 1838), 2: 42.

89. Appleton, "Niagara," in his *Faded Leaves*, pp. 27–30.

90. Richard Lewis Johnson, "Apostrophe to Niagara," in his *Niagara: Its History, Incidents and Poetry* (Washington: Neale, 1898), pp. 35–41; quotation from p. 41.

91. Frank B. Palmer, "Apostrophe to Niagara," in Peter A. Porter, *Official Guide: Niagara Falls, River, Frontier: Scenic, Electric, Historic, Geologic, Hydraulic* (Buffalo: Matthews Northrup Works, 1901), pp. 289–90; quotation from p. 289.

92. Ibid., p. 290.

93. James Warner Ward, "To Niagara," in *Niagara River and Falls* (Buffalo: Thomas F. Fryer, 1886), plate 103.

94. Stowe, letter to her parents, in Fields, *Life and Letters of Harriet Beecher Stowe*, p. 89.

95. Thomas Grinfield, "Hymn on Niagara," in Barham, *Descriptions*, pp. 176–77; quotation from p. 177.

96. Archbishop Lynch, Pastoral letter, in Severance, *Peace Episodes*, p. 107. See also Fleming, *Four Days at the Falls*: Peter A. Porter, "A Legend of Goat Island," ascribed to Hennepin (Niagara Falls, N.Y.: Gazette Press, 1900); H.M.D., "The Falls of Niagara," *Western Literary Messenger*, August 17, 1842, p. 56; and Mrs. C. J. Moreton, "Niagara below the Cataract," in her *Miscellaneous Poems* (Philadelphia: Porter and Coates, 1875), pp. 165–69.

97. Houghton, "Niagara," in his *Niagara and Other Poems*, p. 17.

98. Henry T. Blake, "Niagara: Monarch Supreme in Nature's Glorious Realms" (Hartford: Connecticut Magazine Company, 1903).

99. For example, Howell, "Niagara," in his *Poems* (New York: by author, 1867), p. 198; J. Wellsteed, "The Falls of Niagara," *Western Literary Messenger* 12 (July 1849): 232; Wallace Bruce, "Niagara," in *Michigan Central Railroad* (Chicago: Michigan Central Railroad, 1901), p. 33.

100. Henry Austin, *Independent*, November 29, 1900, p. 2827.

101. Genesis 9:1–16.

102. Greville J. Chester, *Transatlantic Sketches in the West Indies, South America, Canada, and the United States* (London: Smith, Elder, 1869), pp. 280–81.

103. Charles Dickens, *American Notes for General Circulation* (London: Chapman and Hall, 1843), pp. 177–78; see also Chester, "Hymn on Niagara," in Barham, *Descriptions*, p. 176.

104. Lynch, Pastoral letter, in Severance, *Peace Episodes*, p. 104.

105. Ibid., pp. 99, 100.

106. "Aladdin Quite Outdone: Giant Palace to Span the Mighty Niagara Cataract," *New York World*, February 9, 1896; see chap. 5 for further discussion of Henkle's plan.

107. Similar utopian plans were advanced by King C. Gillette, in *The Human Drift* (1894, Boston, New Era Publishing Co.; reprint ed., Delmar, N.Y.: Scholars' Facsimiles and Reprints, 1976; and also by William T. Love in 1893. See Adeline G. Levine, *Love Canal* (Lexington, Mass.: D. C. Heath and Co., 1982); also see Edward Dean Adams, *Niagara Power,* 2 vols. (Niagara Falls, N.Y.: Niagara Falls Power Company, 1927), 1: 97. Much earlier (1825), a "City of Refuge for the Jews" was planned by Mordecai Manuel Noah, "Ararat," *Niagara Gazette,* January 18, 1976, p. 17.

108. Executive Committee to Promote Navy Island as Permanent Headquarters of the United Nations, "Proposed United Nations Headquarters: Navy Island, Niagara Falls," 1945.

109. Sir Angus Fletcher, quoted in Lloyd Graham, *Niagara Country* (New York: Duell, Sloan and Pearce, 1949), p. 6.

110. Graham, *Niagara Country,* p. 293.

111. Severance, *Peace Episodes,* pp. 79–96.

112. Ibid., pp. 3–78.

113. Liston, "Niagara Falls," p. 89.

114. Rev. John Dowling, "Sacred Musings," in *Album of the Table Rock, Niagara Falls* (Buffalo: Jewett, Thomas and Company, 1848), pp. 31–32.

115. Lynch, Pastoral letter, in Severance, *Peace Episodes,* p. 106.

116. Clayton Mau, *The Development of Central and Western New York* (Rochester: Du Bois Press, 1944), p. 8.

117. Frank H. Severance, *An Old Frontier of France,* 2 vols., Publications of the Buffalo Historical Society 21 (Buffalo: Buffalo Historical Society, 1917), 2:303–28.

118. Robert West Howard, *Thundergate: The Forts of Niagara* (Englewood Cliffs, N.J.: Prentice-Hall, 1968), p. 190; and Seibel, *Niagara Falls, Canada,* p. 22.

119. Edwin C. Guillet, *The Lives and Times of the Patriots* (Toronto: Thomas Nelson and Sons, 1938); also Orrin Edward Tiffany, "Relations of the United States to the Canadian Rebellion of 1837–1838," in Frank H. Severance, ed., *Publications of the Buffalo Historical Society* 8 (Buffalo: Buffalo Historical Society, 1905), pp. 1–148.

120. Howard, *Thundergate,* p. 206; Graham, *Niagara Country,* pp. 136–51.

121. Lord Morpeth, "Niagara Falls," in Longfellow, *Poems of Places,* p. 155.

4. The Nature of Niagara

1. James Dixon, *Personal Narrative of a Tour through a Part of the United States and Canada* (New York: Lane and Scott, 1849), p. 125.

2. Unsigned epigram from *The Album of the Table Rock, Niagara Falls* (Buffalo: Jewett, Thomas and Co., 1848), p. 44.

3. Edward Hartley, "The Falls of Niagara" (Toronto: D. D. Dewart, n.d.).

4. Dixon, *Narrative of a Tour*, p. 123.

5. Ralph Waldo Emerson, *Nature, the Collected Works of Ralph Waldo Emerson*, vol. 1 (1836; reprint ed., Cambridge, Mass.: Harvard University Press, 1971), pp. 7–45; quotation from pp. 8–9.

6. Mrs. Frances Milton Trollope, *Domestic Manners of the Americans* (London: Whitaker, Treacher, 1832), p. 303.

7. Anonymous, *Legend of the Whirlpool* (Buffalo: Press of Thomas and Co., 1840).

8. James C. Carter, "Oration at the Dedication of the State Reservation at Niagara, July 15, 1885, "Nineteenth Annual Report of the Commissioners of the State Reservation at Niagara" (Albany: State of New York, 1903), pp. 263–67; reprinted in Charles Mason Dow, *Anthology and Bibliography of Niagara Falls*, 2 vols. (Albany: State of New York, 1921), 2: 1118–28; quotation from p. 1118.

9. Northrop Frye, *The Secular Scripture: A Study of the Structure of Romance* (Cambridge, Mass.: Harvard University Press, 1976), p. 60.

10. James Silk Buckingham, *The Eastern and Western States of America* (London: Fisher, Son, 1843), 3: 458.

11. Emerson, *Nature*, p. 10.

12. Leo Marx, *The Machine in the Garden: Technology and the Pastoral Ideal in America* (New York: Oxford University Press, 1964), p. 286.

13. Rev. Fr. Nerses Baboorian, *O Niagara Our Falls: Epic Poem and History* (Beirut, Lebanon: by author, 1974).

14. James Warner Ward, "To Niagara," in his *Niagara River and Falls* (Buffalo: Thomas F. Fryer, 1886), plate 103.

15. James Silk Buckingham, "Hymn to Niagara," in *Descriptions of Niagara*, ed. William Barham (Gravesend: The Compiler, n.d.), p. 42.

16. Katherine Lee Bates, "The Song of Niagara," *Canadian Magazine*, May 1910, p. 58.

17. Anonymous, untitled, in *Goat Island*, ed. Peter A. Porter (Niagara Falls, N.Y.: n.p., 1900), p. 4.

18. Samuel Langhorne Clemens (Mark Twain), *Extracts from Adams Diary* (1893, Underhill and Nichols; reprint ed., London and New York: Harper and Brothers, 1904), p. 5.

19. Ibid., p. 19.

20. Richard Lewis Johnson, "Apostrophe to Niagara," in his *Niagara: Its History, Incidents and Poetry* (Washington: Walter Neale, 1898), pp. 35–41; quotation from p. 39.

21. John W. Montclair, "Niagara," *Real and Ideal* (Philadelphia, 1865), pp. 49–50; quotation from p. 50.

22. Theodora Vinal, *Niagara Portage* (Buffalo: Foster and Stewart, 1949), p. 39.

23. Isabella Lucy Bird, *The Englishwoman in America* (1856, John Murray of London; reprint ed., Toronto: University of Toronto Press, 1966), p. 223.

24. Barham, *Descriptions,* p. 23.

25. John C. Lord, "The Genius of Niagara," in his *Occasional Poems* (Buffalo: Breed and Lent, 1869), pp. 19–22; quotation from p. 21.

26. "Niagara," Mrs. Lydia Huntley Sigourney, in her *Scenes in My Native Land* (Boston: James Monroe, 1845), pp. 148–61; quotation from p. 148.

27. Henry Howard Brownell, "Niagara," in his *Poems* (New York: D. Appleton and Co., 1847), pp. 35–48; quotation from p. 38.

28. John Douglas Southerland, The Marquis of Lorne (and Duke of Argyll), "Niagara," in his *Memories of Canada and Scotland* (Montreal: Dawson Brothers, 1884), p. 60.

29. Anonymous, *Legend of the Whirlpool* (Buffalo: Thomas & Co., 1840), p. 5.

30. John Edward Howell, in his *Poems,* 2 vols. (New York: by author, 1867), 1: 209.

31. Fredrika Bremer, *The Homes of the New World,* 2 vols. (London: Chapman and Hall, 1850), 2: 196, 202.

32. William Dean Howells, *Their Wedding Journey* (Boston and New York: Houghton, Mifflin and Co., 1888), p. 312.

33. Francis Lieber, *The Stranger in America: Comprising Sketches of the Manners, Society, and National Peculiarities of the United States in a Series of Letters to a Friend in Europe* (London: Richard Bentley, 1835), p. 307.

34. Herman Melville, *Moby Dick* (New York: Library Publications, 1930), pp. 261–62.

35. Charles Dudley Warner, *Their Pilgrimage* (New York: Harper Brothers, 1897), p. 306; George Houghton, "Niagara," in his *Niagara and Other Poems* (Boston: Houghton, Mifflin and Co., 1882), pp. 7–28; quotation from p. 15; Lord, "The Genius of Niagara," in his *Occasional Poems,* p. 19; James C. Carter, "Oration at the Dedication of the State Reservation at Niagara, July 15, 1885," *Nineteenth Annual Report of the Commissioners of the State Reservation at Niagara* (Albany: State of New York, 1903), pp. 263–77, reprinted in Dow, *Anthology,* 2:1118–28; quotation from p. 1119.

36. Warner, *Their Pilgrimage,* p. 304.

37. Ibid., p. 306.

38. Alfred Dommett, *The Canadian Journal of Alfred Domett: Being an Extract from a Journal of a Tour in Canada, the United States and Jamaica, 1833–35* (London, Ontario: University of Western Ontario, 1955), p. 63.

39. Anthony Trollope, *North America* (New York: Harper & Brothers, 1862), p. 93.

40. Harriet Beecher Stowe, letter to her parents in Cincinnati, in *Life and Letters of Harriet Beecher Stowe,* ed. Annie Field (Boston and New York: Houghton, Mifflin and Co., 1897), p. 90.

41. William Fleming, *Four Days at the Falls of Niagara* (n.p.: Gillett Printer, 1885), p. 24.

42. James Knox Liston, *Niagara Falls: A Poem in Three Cantos* (Toronto: for author by J. H. Lawrence, Printer, 1843), p. 88.

43. Isabella Bird, *An Englishwomen in America,* pp. 218–19.

44. Walter Gore Marshall, *Through America or Nine Months in the United States* (London: Sampson Low, Marston, Searle & Rivington, 1881), p. 77.

45. R. E. Garczynaki, "Niagara," in *Picturesque America,* ed. William Cullen Bryant (New York: D. Appleton and Co., 1872), 1: 432–51; quotation from pp. 434–35.

46. Trollope, *North America,* p. 94.

47. George William Curtis, *Lotus-Eating: A Summer Book* (New York: Harper Brothers, 1852), p. 100.

48. Evelyn Watson, "The Peace Bridge," in her *Poems of the Niagara Frontier* (New York: Dean and Co., 1929), pp. 101–2; quotation from p. 101.

49. Watson, "The Power Plant," in her *Poems of the Niagara Frontier,* p. 83.

50. Liston, "Niagara Falls," p. 55.

51. Edward Zaremba, "Niagara Captive," *Metallurgical and Chemical Engineer,* March 1913, p. 120.

52. Carter, "Oration at the Dedication," in Dow, *Anthology,* 2:1118.

53. Howells, *Their Wedding Journey,* pp. 165–66.

54. Mrs. Anna Brownell Jameson, *Winter Studies and Summer Rambles in Canada,* 3 vols. (London: Saunders and Otley, 1838), 2: 64.

55. Leo Marx, *Machine in the Garden,* p. 291.

56. Watson, "Niagara in Winter," in her *Poems of the Niagara Frontier,* pp. 43–45; quotation from p. 45.

57. Arnold Hauser, "A Flight from Reality," in *Romanticism: Definition, Explanation, and Evaluation,* ed. John B. Halsted (Boston: D. C. Heath and Co., 1965), pp. 67–76; quotation from p. 72.

58. F. L. Lucas, *Decline and Fall of the Romantic Ideal* (New York: Macmillan, 1937), pp. 31–32.

59. D. M. Thomas, "Author's Note," *The White Hotel* (New York: The Viking Press, 1981), p. vii.

60. Carter, "Oration at the Dedication," in Dow, *Anthology,* 2:1120.

61. Thomas Cole, Reflections after His Second Visit, September 4, 1847, in *The Course of Empire, Voyage of Life, and Other Pictures of Thomas Cole, N.A.: With Selections from His Letters and Miscellaneous Writings,* ed. Louis L. Noble (New York: Cornish, Lampart, and Co., 1853), pp. 376–77.

62. Benjamin Copeland, "Niagara," in his *Niagara and Other Poems* (Buffalo: Matthews-Northrup, 1904), pp. 11–12; quotation from p. 12.

63. Caroline Gilman, *The Poetry of Travelling in the United States* (New York: S. Colman, 1838), p. 116.

64. Sigmund Freud, *A General Introduction to Psychoanalysis,* trans. Joan Riviere (Garden City, N.Y.: Garden City Publishing Co., 1943), pp. 23–24, 302.

65. C. G. Jung, *The Archetypes and the Collective Unconscious,* trans. R.F.C. Hull, vol. 9, part 1 of *Works of C. G. Jung* (Princeton, N.J.: Princeton University Press, 1964), p. 142.

66. Fleming, *Four Days at the Falls,* p. 24.

67. William Dean Howells, "Niagara, First and Last," in his *The Niagara Book* (Buffalo: Underhill and Nichols, 1893), p. 22.

68. George Seibel, ed., *Niagara Falls, Canada: A History* (Niagara Falls, Ontario: Kiwanis Club of Stamford, Ontario, 1967), pp. 49–51; Liston, in "Niagara Falls," called it "depraved," p. 57.

69. James Bird, *Francis Abbott: The Recluse of Niagara* (London: Baldwin and Cradock, 1837), p. 67.

70. Ibid., pp. 70–71.

71. Richard Watson Gilder, "To Niagara," in his *Poems* (Boston and New York: Houghton, Mifflin and Co., 1908), pp. 215–16; quotation is from p. 216.

72. Henry Hathaway, director, *Niagara;* produced by Charles Brackett; written by Charles Brackett, Walter Reisch, and Richard Breen; released by 20th Century-Fox, 1953; starring Marilyn Monroe, Joseph Cotten, and Jean Peters.

73. A reproduction of this poster from the collection of Karl Schmutzler recently appeared in an article by Gary Walther, "Niagara Souvenirs: One Man's Love Affair with Kitsch," *Smithsonian,* January 1984, pp. 106–11; quotation is from p. 111; Mrs. Humphrey Ward produced a similar story of marital infelicity at Niagara in her *Marriage à la Mode* (New York: Doubleday, Page and Co., 1909).

74. Genesis 9:18–28.

75. Henry Tudor, *Narrative of a Tour in North America* (London: James Duncan, 1834), p. 239.

76. J. Wellsteed, "The Falls of Niagara," *Western Literary Messenger,* July 1849, p. 232; see also Liston, "Niagara Falls," p. 93, when he asks God to lull his "warring passions" and then identifies them with "wild imagination" which confuses and bewilders the brain.

77. Niagara Falls became a popular honeymoon resort with the completion of the New York Central in 1853. At least as early as 1839, however, many honeymooners were traveling to Niagara. See Walter McCausland, "Honeymooners at Niagara Falls," *American Notes and Queries,* November 1946, pp. 122–23; see also Marjorie F. Williams's letter to Walter Pilkington, editor of *American Notes and Queries,* Historical Collection, Niagara Falls (N.Y.) Public Library, 1946.

78. Howell, "Niagara," in his *Poems,* p. 215.

79. An interpretation arrived at independently in Elizabeth McKinsey, *Ni-*

agara Falls: Icon of the American Sublime (New York: Cambridge University Press, 1985), p. 188; and in Patrick McGreevy, "Visions at the Brink; Imagination and the Geography of Niagara Falls" (Ph.D. diss., University of Minnesota, 1984), p. 187.

80. See also Liston, "Niagara Falls," Canto I; Johnson, "Apostrophe to Niagara," in his *Niagara*.

81. See Gordon Donaldson, *Niagara!: The Eternal Circus* (New York: Doubleday, 1979), pp. 9–11; and Frank H. Severance, *Peace Episodes on the Niagara* (Publications Buffalo Historical Society, 1914), p. 108n.

82. William Trumbull, "The Legend of the White Canoe" (New York and London: G. P. Putnam's Sons, 1894), pp. 1–3.

83. Houghton, "Niagara," in his *Niagara and Other Poems*, p. 10.

84. Williard Parker, *Niagara's Rainbow: The Legend of the White Canoe* (Conshohocken, Pa.: Willard Publishing Co., 1922).

85. Michael Butor, *Niagara*, trans. Elinor S. Miller (1965, France; reprint ed., Chicago: Henry Regnery Co., 1969).

86. Richard Gilman, "Total Revolution in the Novel," *Horizon* 4, no. 3 (January 1962): 96–101; see also Germaine Baril, ed., *Butor Studies*, special issue of *Kentucky Romance Quarterly* 32 (February 1985): 1.

87. François Auguste René Chateaubriand (Paris: Impr. de Migneret, an 9, 1801).

88. Butor, *Niagara*, pp. 15, 16, 131.

89. Ibid., p. 70.

90. Ibid., pp. 245, 102, 91–92, 176, 96, 133.

91. Ibid., pp. 126, 96, 97.

92. Ibid., pp. 175, 70.

93. Oscar Wilde, *Impressions of America* (1883; reprint ed., Sunderland: Keystone Press, 1906), p. 25.

5. The Future of Niagara

1. James Dixon, *Personal Narrative of a Tour Through a Part of the United States and Canada* (New York: Lane and Scott, 1849), pp. 121–22.

2. Anonymous, "Niagara," *Godey's Ladys Book and Magazine*, September 1861, p. 348.

3. I. F. Clarke, *The Pattern of Expectation, 1644–2001* (New York: Basic Books, 1979), p. 7.

4. Bernard McGinn, *Visions of the End: Apocalyptic Traditions in the Middle Ages* (New York: Columbia University Press, 1979), p. 36.

5. Charles Beard, "Introduction" to J. B. Bury, *An Inquiry into the Idea of Progress* (1932, Macmillan Co.; reprint ed., New York: Dover Publications, 1955), p. xi.

6. Clarence Glacken, *Traces on the Rhodian Shore: Nature and Culture in Western Thought from Ancient Times to the End of the Eighteenth Century* (Berkeley: University of California Press, 1967), p. 473.

7. Francis Bacon, *Novum Organum* (1620; reprint ed., New York: P. F. Collier & Son, 1901), bk. 1, aph. 129.

8. Francis Bacon, *The New Atlantis*, ed. Henry Morley (1629; reprint ed., New York: P. F. Collier & Son, 1901), p. 129.

9. Bury, *Idea of Progress*, pp. 98–126.

10. Edward Cornish, *The Study of the Future* (Washington: World Future Society, 1977), pp. 58–60.

11. Bury, *Idea of Progress*, p. 324.

12. Edward Bellamy, *Looking Backward, 2000–1887* (Boston: Ticknor, 1888).

13. Cornish, *Study of the Future*, p. 64.

14. Kenneth Roemer, *The Obsolete Necessity: America in Utopian Writings, 1888–1900* (Kent, Ohio: Kent State University Press, 1976), p. 177.

15. Ibid., p. 19.

16. Bury, *Idea of Progress*, p. 324.

17. Albert, the Prince Consort, *Times* (London), April 30, 1851, quoted in Bury, *Idea of Progress*, p. 330.

18. Harry L. Goldman, "Nikola Tesla's Bold Adventure," *American West*, March 1971, pp. 4–9.

19. Glen C. Forrester, *Niagara Falls and the Glacier* (Hicksville, N.Y.: Exposition Press, 1976), p. 125; Theodora Vinal, *Niagara Portage* (Buffalo: Foster and Stewart, 1949), pp. 101–102.

20. Benjamin Copeland, "Niagara," in his *Niagara and Other Poems* (Buffalo: Mathews-Northrup, 1904), pp. 11–12.

21. Duke of Liancourt, *Travels Through the United States of North America, the Country of the Iroquois, and Upper Canada, in the Years 1795, 1796, and 1797*, 2 vols. (London: R. Phillips, 1799), 1: 221.

22. See, for example, Charles Dudley Warner, *Their Pilgrimage* (New York: Harper Brothers, 1886), p. 313; Ernest A. Le Sueur, "Commercial Power Development at Niagara," *Popular Science Monthly* 45 (September 1894): 608–30, quotation from p. 609; Augustus Porter and P. B. Porter, "Invitation to Eastern Capitalists and Manufacturers," June 25, 1825, reprinted in Edward Dean Adams, *Niagara Power: History of the Niagara Falls Power Company*, 2 vols. (Niagara Falls, N.Y.: n.p., 1927), 1: 375–76; Augustus Porter, "To Capitalists and Manufacturers," January 1847, reprinted in Adams, *Niagara Power*, 1: 377.

23. Vinal, *Niagara Portage*, p. 23; William Pierson Judson, "History of the Various Projects, Reports, Discussions and Estimates for Reaching the Great Lakes from Tide-Water, 1768–1901," 1901, quoted in Charles Mason Dow, *Anthology and Bibliography of Niagara Falls*, 2 vols. (Albany: State of New York, 1921), 2: 1247–49; quotation from p. 1247.

24. Vinal, *Niagara Portage*, p. 24; Judson, "History of the Various Projects," quoted in Dow, *Anthology*, 2: 1247; Frank H. Severance, "Historical Sketch of the Board of Trade, the Merchant's Exchange, and the Chamber of Commerce of Buffalo," *Publications of the Buffalo Historical Society*, 13: 311–13.

25. F. R. Delano, *The Water Power of Niagara* (New York: Banker's Publishing Association, 1881), p. 4.

26. A. Porter, "To Capitalists," reprinted in Adams, *Niagara Power*, 1: 377.

27. Adams, *Niagara Power*, 1: 48, 375.

28. Porter and Porter, "Invitation to Eastern Capitalists," reprinted in ibid., 1: 375.

29. Quoted in Adams, *Niagara Power* 1: 74.

30. Adams, *Niagara Power* 1: 76–82.

31. *Report of the International Joint Commission, United States and Canada, on the Preservation and Enhancement of Niagara Falls* (Washington and Ottawa: 1953), p. 348.

32. Evershed's original scheme and the plan finally implemented are outlined in Adams, *Niagara Power*, 1: 115–92, 233–332; *Report of the Special International Niagara Board on the Preservation and Improvement of Niagara Falls and Rapids* (Washington: U.S. Government Printing Office, 1931); Gordon Donaldson, *Niagara!: The Eternal Circus* (New York: Doubleday, 1979), pp. 212–15; Hamilton B. Mizer, *Niagara Falls: A Topical History, 1892–1932* (Lockport, N.Y.: Niagara County Historical Society, 1981), p. 49; Vinal, *Niagara Portage*, pp. 93–101; O. A. Kenyon, "Rise of Niagara Power," *Electric World and Engineer* 46 (1905): 654–56.

33. Adams, *Niagara Power*, 1: 116.

34. Ibid., 1: 141–60.

35. Ibid., 1: 181–92.

36. Ibid., 1: 214; *Report on Preservation and Improvement*, p. 28.

37. See map in Adams, *Niagara Power*, 1: 321–22.

38. Canadian power development is reviewed in *Report on Preservation and Improvement*, pp. 350–54; Kenyon, "Rise of Niagara Power," p. 656; Donaldson, *Niagara!*, pp. 217–20; George Seibel, *Niagara Falls, Canada: A History* (Niagara Falls, Ontario: Kiwanis Club of Stamford, Ontario, 1967), pp. 364–74.

39. Seibel, *Niagara Falls, Canada*, p. 366.

40. Ibid., pp. 368–69; Donaldson, *Niagara!*, p. 219; see map in Adams, *Niagara Power*, 2: 136.

41. See tables in *Report on Preservation and Improvement*, pp. 349, 353, 354.

42. Sylvanus Phillips Thompson, *Life of William Thompson, Baron Kelvin of Largs*, 2 vols. (London: Macmillan, 1910), quoted in Dow, *Anthology*, 2: 1042.

43. Frederick Law Olmsted and Calvert Vaux, "General Plan for the Improvement of Niagara Reservation," in *Supplemental Report of the Commissioners*

of the State Reservation at Niagara (Albany: State of New York, 1887), pp. 9–50, quoted in Dow, *Anthology*, 2: 1131.

44. Mary B. Hartt, "The Passing of Niagara," *Outlook*, May 4, 1901, pp. 21–28; quotation is from p. 21.

45. French Strother, "Shall Niagara Be Saved?" *World's Work* 12 (May 1906): 7524–35.

46. Alton D. Adams, "The Destruction of Niagara Falls," *Cassier's* 27 (March 1905): 413–17; see also his "Vandalism at Niagara Falls," *Scientific American*, April 15, 1905.

47. "National Park at Niagara Falls," letter submitted to Congress by the secretary of war, December 21, 1909 (U.S. Congress, 2d Session, House Document 431, serial 5834).

48. Adams, *Niagara Power*, 1: 206.

49. Ibid., 1: 215–16.

50. Ibid., 1: 223.

51. *Report on Preservation and Improvement*, pp. 348–49.

52. Adams, *Niagara Power*, 1: 353.

53. Le Sueur, "Commercial Power Development," p. 612; see also A. Howell Van Cleve, "Utilization of Water Power at Niagara," *Bulletin of the Buffalo Society of Natural Science* 8, no. 1 (March 1903): 3–20; quotation from p. 5.

54. Van Cleve, "Niagara Power," p. 10.

55. Walden Fawcett, "The New Niagara," *American Manufacturing and Iron World*, December 25, 1902, pp. 717–20; "The New Niagara," *Harper's Weekly*, January 3, 1903, p. 1.

56. Adams, *Niagara Power*, 1, frontispiece.

57. Ibid., page preceding frontispiece.

58. George William Curtis, *Lotus-Eating: A Summer Book* (New York: Harper and Brothers, 1852), p. 100.

59. Vinal, *Niagara Portage*, p. 90; Kenyon, "Rise of Niagara Power," p. 654.

60. Henry F. Pringle and Katherine Pringle, "The Cities of America: Niagara Falls," *Saturday Evening Post*, October 30, 1948, p. 94; "Lavish Palace Half-Mile Long Once Proposed for the Falls," *Buffalo Evening News*, October 21, 1946.

61. Adams, *Niagara Power*, 1: 93–95; see also "Scheme for the Electrical Utilization of Niagara," *Electric World*, February 9, 1889, pp. 71–72.

62. Adams, *Niagara Power*, 1: 95.

63. There are several other proposals that I will not discuss, for example, John Trowbridge, "Niagara the Motor for the World's Fair," *The Chautauquan* 14, no. 4 (January 1892): 441–45; Alton D. Adams, "Niagara Power at Goat Island," *Scientific American*, November 15, 1905, p. 295.

64. Adams, *Niagara Power*, 1: 96–97; Michael Brown, *Laying Waste: The*

Poisoning of America by Toxic Chemicals (New York: Pantheon Books, 1979), pp. 7–8; Adeline Gordon Levine, *Love Canal: Science, Politics, and People* (Lexington, Mass.: Lexington Books, D. C. Heath and Co., 1982), p. 9; *Model City Bulletin* 1, no. 1 (August 10, 1895).

65. Adams, *Niagara Power*, 1: 96.

66. Levine, *Love Canal*, p. 9.

67. Brown, *Laying Waste*, p. 8.

68. *Model City Bulletin*, p. 12.

69. Adams, *Niagara Power*, 1: 96.

70. *Model City Bulletin*, p. 12.

71. Adams, *Niagara Power*, 1: 96.

72. Ibid., 1: 96.

73. Brown, *Laying Waste*, p. 8; Levine, *Love Canal*, p. 9; "An Act to Incorporate the Model Town Company," 1893, and amendment, 1894, are described in Dow, *Anthology*, 2: 1134–35.

74. Levine, *Love Canal*, p. 9; Adams, *Niagara Power*, p. 97.

75. King Camp Gillette, *The Human Drift* (1894, New Era Publishing Co.; reprint ed., Delmar, N.Y.: Scholar's Facsimiles & Reprints, 1976), with an introduction by Kenneth Roemer.

76. Roemer, "Introduction," *The Human Drift*.

77. Ibid., p. xv.

78. Ibid., p. xv.

79. Ibid., p. vii.

80. These include: *The Ballot Box*, a pamphlet, 1897; "World Corporation (Unlimited)," *National Magazine*, 1906; *World Corporation* (Boston: The New England News Co., 1910); *The People's Corporation* (New York: Boni and Liveright, 1924).

81. Gillette, *Human Drift*, pp. 75, 79, 71, 131.

82. Gillette, *World Corporation*, p. 240.

83. Gillette, *Human Drift*, p. 63; see also *World Corporation*, p. 224.

84. Gillette, *Human Drift*, p. 84.

85. Gillette, *World Corporation*, p. 95.

86. Gillette, *Human Drift*, pp. 24, 87.

87. Ibid., p. 75.

88. Ibid., pp. 87, v, 69.

89. Ibid., pp. 88, 108.

90. Ibid., pp. 53, 70, 130, 67.

91. Ibid., pp. 47, 117, 71, 84, 89.

92. Ibid., p. 75.

93. Gillette, *World Corporation*, pp. 232–33.

94. Roemer, *The Obsolete Necessity*, pp. 232–33.

95. Gillette, *Human Drift*, pp. 90–91, 107–9, 85.

96. Gillette, Human Drift, pp. 92–93.

97. Gillette, *People's Corporation,* p. 167.

98. Ibid., pp. 89, 93, 109, 63.

99. Ibid., p. 86.

100. Ibid., p. 60.

101. Ibid., pp. 112, 75.

102. Aladdin Quite Outdone: Giant Palace to Span the Mighty Niagara,"
The World, February 9, 1896; "A Huge Structure: Leonard Henkle's Plan to
Bridge the Niagara River," *Union and Advertiser,* May 4, 1895, p. 43; "Lavish
Palace Half-Mile Long Once Proposed for the Falls," *Buffalo Evening News,*
October 21, 1946.

103. Aladdin Outdone," *World.*

104. "A Huge Structure," *Union and Advertiser.*

105. Van Cleve, "Utilization of Water Power," p. 20.

106. Gaunault Agassiz, "Niagara—the 'Mighty Thunderer,'" *National
Magazine,* September 1912, pp. 711–34; quotation from p. 713.

107. Thomas H. Norton, "Niagara on Tap," *Popular Science Monthly* 88
(February 1916): 180–84.

108. H. G. Wells, "The End of Niagara," in his *The Future in America*
(Leipzig: Bernhard Tauchnitz, 1907), pp. 60–66; also published in *Harper's
Weekly,* July 21, 1906, pp. 1018–20.

109. Ibid., pp. 60–62.

110. Ibid., pp. 63, 64.

111. Ibid., pp. 64–65.

112. Howell, "Niagara," in *Poems,* p. 203; Harriet Beecher Stowe, "Impres-
sions of a Visit Made in the Summer of 1834," in *Life and Letters of Harriet
Beecher Stowe,* ed. Annie Fields (Boston: Houghton, Mifflin, 1897), pp. 89–90;
Henry Tudor, *Narrative of a Tour in North America,* 2 vols. (London: James
Duncan, 1834), 1: 266; H.D.M., "The Falls of Niagara," *Western Literary
Messenger* 2 (August 17, 1842): 56; John C. Lord, "The Genius of Niagara," in
his *Occasional Poems* (Buffalo: Breed and Lent, 1869), pp. 19–22.

113. Raymond Williams, *Culture and Society, 1780–1950* (New York: Columbia University Press, 1958).

114. Thomas Carlyle, *Shooting Niagara: And After?* (London: Chapman and
Hall, 1867).

115. Clarke, *Pattern of Expectation,* pp. 7, 146.

116. Carlyle, *Shooting Niagara,* p. 16.

117. Thomas Carlyle, "Signs of the Times," *Edinburgh Review* (1829),
quoted in Williams, *Culture and Society,* p. 73; see chap. 4, "Thomas Carlyle,"
pp. 71–86.

118. Carlyle, *Shooting Niagara,* pp. 2, 22–23, 11.

119. Ibid., pp. 24–25, 51–53.

120. Jules Verne, *The Master of the World,* in *Works of Jules Verne,* ed. Charles F. Horne, vol. 14 (London and New York: Vincent Parke and Company, 1911).

121. Ibid., p. 143.

122. Ibid., pp. 200–201.

123. Ibid., pp. 237–38.

124. Ibid., p. 252.

125. Ibid., pp. 249–58.

126. H. G. Wells, *The War in the Air* (London: George Bell and Sons, 1908).

127. Ibid., p. 335.

128. Ibid., p. 251.

129. Ibid., p. 273.

130. Ibid., pp. 250, 345, 349, 355.

131. Ibid., p. 272.

132. Ibid., p. 371.

133. Clarke, *Pattern of Expectation, 1644–2001* (New York: Basic Books, 1979), p. 227.

134. Ibid., p. 295.

135. Robert C. Dille, *The Collected Works of Buck Rogers in the 25th Century* (New York: Chelsea House Publications, 1962).

136. Ibid., p. 23, strip #91.

137. Mizer, *Niagara Falls,* p. 100; A. E. Coombs, *History of the Niagara Peninsula and the New Welland Canal* (Toronto: Historical Publications Association, 1930), pp. 88–89.

138. "Peace Ceremonies at Cataract," *Buffalo Express,* June 9, 1925, p. 1; "Border Neighbors Renew Friendship at Dedication of Falls Lighting," *Buffalo Express,* June 9, 1925, p. 4.

139. Mizer, *Niagara Falls,* p. 100; "Magnificent Display," *Buffalo Courier,* June 9, 1925, p. 4.

140. Mizer, *Niagara Falls,* pp. 100, 102.

141. "Proposed United Nations Headquarters: Navy Island, Niagara Falls," submitted to the Executive Committee of the United Nations by the Executive Committee of the International Committee to Promote Navy Island as Permanent Headquarters of the United Nations, 1945.

142. Pringle and Pringle, "Niagara Falls."

143. Robert McNamee, "Onaguiaahra," *Michigan Quarterly Review,* February 1962, p. 41; *Preservation and Enhancement,* p. 18.

144. Ibid.

145. Forrester, *Niagara Falls and the Glacier,* p. 134.

146. *Preservation and Enhancement,* plate 3, p. 39.

147. R. B. MacMullin, F. L. Koethen, and C. N. Richardson, "Chemical

Industry on the Niagara Frontier," *Transactions of the American Institute of Chemical Engineers* 36(1940): 295–324.

148. "Chemical Progress in Niagara Falls," *The Tapping Pot,* Union Carbide and Carbon Corporation, Electro Metallurgical Company 23, no. 4 (May 1954):9.

149. "Proposal for National Accelerator Laboratory," submitted to the U.S. Atomic Energy Commission by the Society for the Promotion, Unification and Redevelopment of Niagara, Inc., Niagara Falls, New York, 1965.

150. Robert Panero, with Basil Candela and William McGuigan, "Niagara Falls, New York: An Appraisal of the City," Hudson Institute Paper H1-1099-P, September 23, 1968.

151. Brown, *Laying Waste;* Levine, *Love Canal.*

Conclusion

1. François Auguste René Chateaubriand, *Travels in America and Italy* (London: Colburn, 1828), 1: 131–34; quotation from p. 132.

2. Nathaniel Hawthorne, "My Visit to Niagara," in his *Tales, Sketches, and Other Papers* (1850; reprint ed., Boston: Houghton, Mifflin, 1883), pp. 42–50; quotation from p. 45.

3. George Seibel, ed., *Niagara Falls, Canada: A History* (Niagara Falls, Ontario: Kiwanis Club of Stamford, Ontario, 1967), p. 395.

INDEX